COVENANT DISCIPLESHIP

Christian Formation through Mutual Accountability

W9-BDM-812

David Lowes Watson

DISCIPLESHIP RESOURCES
MATERIALS FOR GROWTH IN CHRISTIAN FAITH & LIFE
— NASHVILLE, TENNESSEE —
P.O. BOX 840 • NASHVILLE, TN 37202 • PHONE (615) 340-7068

Reprinted 1996.

Library of Congress Catalog Card No. 90-82418

ISBN 0-88177-091-4

DR091

*To my wife, Gayle, for her
unfailing support in the
work of covenant discipleship,
and now for the profound assurance
of joining me in the ministry
of word and sacrament.*

Contents

Acknowledgments

My deepest acknowledgment in preparing this new handbook must be to the many hundreds of congregational leaders, clergy and lay, who have formed covenant discipleship groups in order to hold themselves accountable for their discipleship. In the truest sense, they are the *Methodists* of today, recovering a Wesleyan tradition we have come dangerously close to losing in our present climate of churchly success and religious self-fulfillment.

In addition, I wish to express my thanks to those who have helped to bring covenant discipleship groups to their present stage of development. I continue to be grateful to my colleagues at the General Board of Discipleship: in particular to the General Secretary, Ezra Earl Jones, for his initiative in allowing covenant discipleship to have church-wide opportunities, and for his leadership of the church in many other areas of discipleship; and to Victor Pérez-Silvestry, Associate General Secretary, for his valued administrative support and encouragement.

Most especially I wish to thank my colleagues in the Office of Covenant Discipleship and Christian Formation. Marigene Chamberlain has been pivotal in establishing the office as an integral part of the General Board of Discipleship, and in gaining recognition for our work through her skillful editing of the *Covenant Discipleship Quarterly*, in both English and Spanish. Phyllis Tyler-Wayman has brought her considerable pastoral and connectional expertise to bear on covenant discipleship, resulting in a fresh focus on our priorities. The "General Rule of Discipleship" which features prominently in the following pages owes much to her insistence that Wesley's vocabulary be made accessible to the church of today.

Covenant discipleship has also been significantly shaped by the wisdom and support of two outstanding teachers in our United Methodist schools of theology. Frederick Herzog at Duke Divinity School has been an advocate for our work with true Wesleyan integrity. In forging our guidelines for discipleship, he has never allowed us to forget the imperative of God's justice toward those who comprise two-thirds of our global family. To use his own words, "The world is not our parish—our parish is the world."

Robin Maas has enriched our work by grounding it in the spiritual heritage of the church. Not only has she done this in a number of excellent writings, she has also introduced covenant discipleship into the curriculum of Wesley Theological Seminary, enabling future pastors to integrate their personal spirituality and their theological education.

At Discipleship Resources, the helpful suggestions of Craig B. Gallaway and David L. Hazlewood have greatly improved the text, and the creativity of J. Lee Bonnet is once again evident in the design of the volume. My thanks are also due to Stephen L. Potter for his keen promotion of the project, and to Connie Dillingham for her careful preparation of the manuscript.

Reflecting on the past fifteen years, it is heartening to record that two of the earliest advocates of covenant discipleship are still at the cutting edge of our work. The Rev. Jim Beal, Superintendent of the Batesville District in North Arkansas, and Judge Merrill L. Hartman of the 192nd District Court in Dallas, Texas, are now among our adjunct staff members at the General Board of Discipleship. To them, and the many more who have joined us in returning to the basics of Methodism, my profound thanks for their willingness to be fellow pilgrims, and thereby a constant means of grace.

General Board of Discipleship   November 1990
Nashville, Tennessee

Preface

Lord Jesus, if thou wilt receive me into thine house, if thou wilt but own me as thy servant, I will not stand upon terms; impose upon me what conditions thou pleasest, write down thine own articles, command me what thou wilt, put me to any thing thou seest good; let me be thy servant, and spare not to command me; I will be no longer mine own, but give up myself to thy will in all things.

From John Wesley's Covenant Service, 1780

Introduction
A Wesleyan Tradition

COVENANT DISCIPLESHIP GROUPS

From their beginning in 1975, covenant discipleship groups have followed an important Wesleyan precedent: the early Methodist class meeting. They have followed another Wesleyan precedent in responding to the expressed need of Christians who want to make a deeper commitment to their faith. The groups have now developed to the point where a new handbook is needed, incorporating the learnings of the past fifteen years, and pointing toward a significant new phase of their work: the revitalization of the office of *class leader.*

Appropriately, the first covenant discipleship group was formed in a local congregation: Holly Springs United Methodist Church, North Carolina. The members did not feel they were doing anything particularly significant. They merely wished to be accountable for their discipleship, and to seek the grace of God by practicing the time-honored disciplines of the church. So it was with the early Methodist class meeting, which came about more by accident than design, and which functioned with a minimum of formality and with few regulations. Indeed, the impression we get from Wesley's writings is that directives were far less important than the commitment and practical witness of those who met week by week to "watch over one another in love."

Like the early class meetings, covenant discipleship groups require minimal direction. Those who join are sufficiently committed to their discipleship to have outgrown the need for step-by-step instructions. What they have not outgrown, however, and never will, is the need for accountability. This is what draws them to their weekly meetings with methodical regularity. By centering on the tasks of the Christian life, and giving an account of what they have done during the past week, group members are able to accept one another as fellow disciples. Irrespective of what are often widely differing religious experiences, they find they can support one another in the basics of Christian discipleship.

A NEW HANDBOOK

The first handbook for covenant discipleship groups, *Accountable Discipleship* (Discipleship Resources, 1983), merely expressed in written form what group members were discovering in their weekly meetings. It thus provided a means by which many others discovered the pragmatism and inclusiveness of covenant discipleship. This new handbook, however, has gone further. It is designed not only as an introduction to covenant discipleship groups, but also as a reference guide which can be of help whenever there are questions about the nature and purpose of a group, or of covenant discipleship in general.

THE "WHY" OF COVENANT DISCIPLESHIP

The first five chapters deal with the challenge of Christian discipleship, and why the early Methodist class meeting is so important for the church of today. Each chapter is followed by discussion questions, addressing issues which often arise when people consider joining a covenant discipleship group. If you have made that decision and are now part of a group, some of these issues may be emerging in a new light. It may be helpful to look at them again as you become more involved in your weekly meetings.

THE "HOW" OF COVENANT DISCIPLESHIP

The next three chapters of the book deal with the practical dimensions of covenant discipleship groups: how to get them started, how to write the covenant, how to lead the group meetings, and how to keep them a lively and healthy part of your congregation's ministry and mission. Throughout each chapter, there are helpful suggestions, received from group members over the past fifteen years; and in chapters six and seven, there is a detailed listing of questions which have most frequently been raised as covenant discipleship groups have grown across the United States and in a number of countries around the world. In other words, *Covenant Discipleship* is designed as a handbook in the fullest sense of the word—something to keep "handy" whenever you have questions about your group.

GRACIOUS DISCIPLINE

As you hold yourself accountable for your discipleship week by week, you will be joining many hundreds of faithful church members who are responding to the call of Jesus Christ to become more disciplined in their Christian living. In the months and years which lie ahead, you will find your covenant discipleship group a means of grace, through which God will empower you to live out your discipleship in the world with fresh vigor and dedication. All of this you will discover as your daily walk with Christ becomes more consistent—the privilege and the assurance of being in covenant with God. This in turn will give you a new sense of God's mission and ministry for the church which you can share with the other members of your congregation.

BACK TO BASICS

As Wesley himself acknowledged two hundred years ago, class meetings were not an innovation for the church, but merely the recovery of some basic principles for the practice of Christian discipleship. By the same token, covenant discipleship groups are not new. They are merely a means, or channel, of grace—but a channel which perennially falls into neglect.

It was heartening, therefore, that in 1984 the General Board of Discipleship adopted covenant discipleship as a Bicentennial initiative for The United Methodist Church. This has generated a much wider constituency for the groups, and has given them a growing influence in the ministry and mission of many local congregations.

CLASS LEADERS

Covenant discipleship groups have developed to the point where they are now ready to enter a major new phase in the life and work of the church. They are going to be the means of implementing one of the most significant steps taken by any Methodist denomination in the past hundred years: the re-introduction of the office of *class leader* into the congregational life of The United Methodist Church (*The Book of Discipline*, 1988, para. 268). Accordingly, this new handbook for covenant discipleship groups is one of three new resources. Joining it will be *Class Leaders: Recovering a Tradition* (order no. DR092) and *Forming Christian Disciples: The Role of Covenant Discipleship and Class Leaders in the Congregation* (order no. DR093), published as a trilogy by Discipleship Resources. It is the prayer and hope of those of us at the General Board of Discipleship that these volumes will help to rediscover and re-apply the open secret of our Methodist heritage—methodical, faithful discipleship.

Chapter 1

The Challenge of Christian Discipleship

It has never been easy to be a Christian disciple, and the late twentieth century is no exception. For Christian discipleship—the real thing, that is—demands a radical commitment to Jesus of Nazareth. It means accepting his lifestyle and following his teachings. It means taking seriously what he had to say about the kingdom of God: the coming reign of love, peace, and justice, on earth as in heaven, when the first will be last and the last first, and when the meek, not the strong, will be in charge. Such a commitment is bound to cause tensions with the world. It always has.

THE CALL TO DISCIPLESHIP

The call to discipleship from Jesus is disconcertingly direct, and it usually catches us unawares. We begin the Christian life by accepting the gift of God's salvation. We experience God's forgiveness and reconciliation, and we come to know the deep joy and inward peace of walking with Christ day by day. Through the indwelling Holy Spirit, working in us and through us, we learn the mind of Christ and are assured of his guidance and strength every step of the way. No aspect of our lives, no detail, is too large or too small to place in the hands of the God who is at once our creator, savior, and spiritual counselor.

But then the call of this carpenter from Nazareth arrests our enjoyment of these spiritual benefits and brings us face to face with some obligations. The call is to become one of his disciples; and the more we learn about this man who celebrated at Jewish weddings, who ate Jewish food, who walked the roads of Palestine and who sweated Jewish sweat, the more we find that

1

his invitation to discipleship leaves nothing in doubt, yet everything open.

THE UNCONDITIONAL CONDITION

Jesus stipulates only one condition, but it proves to be unconditional: a trusting obedience. "Follow me," he said to Simon, Andrew, James, and John (Matt. 4:18-22). No trial period to see if they liked it. No discussion about potential benefits. No mention of the prospect of a fulfilled life and personhood. The reward of following this particular rabbi would be neither more nor less than the privilege of sharing in his work.

In due course it would be clear to his followers how rich was that reward; but that would not and could not be their motive for answering his call. The decision to become a disciple of Jesus of Nazareth meant taking an unqualified risk, a willingness to abandon everything the world held to be important for the sake of those things that were of eternal importance. His parables and teachings made that clear time and again: the hidden treasure (Matt. 13:44); the man who built bigger barns (Luke 12:13-21); the prodigal son (Luke 15:11-32); and the harsh directive that following him with integrity would mean neglecting one's family and friends for the sake of the task in hand (Luke 14:26).

The purpose for joining Jesus had to be a sharing of his vision of a new age for this planet and the conviction that he was the one who would bring it to pass. His word for this vision was the *kingdom*, a time when the will of God would indeed be done on earth as in heaven (Matt. 6:10): a new age, when God would truly be acknowledged as God by all people, from the least to the greatest (Jeremiah 31:34); a new age, when the wolf would dwell with the lamb, the leopard would lie down with the kid, the lion would eat straw like the ox, and the earth would be full of the knowledge of God as the waters cover the sea (Isaiah 11:6:9); a new age, of good news for the poor, release for captives, sight for the blind, liberty for the oppressed (Luke 4:18-19; a new age, when there would be neither Jew nor Greek, neither slave nor free, neither male nor female (Galatians 3:28).

And *now* was the time to expect this. The prophetic vision of the future had become a present reality in the person of Jesus Christ.

This new age, this coming reign of God, was at hand *right now* (Luke 4:21).

THE COST OF DISCIPLESHIP

We know that this vision ultimately led to his execution, a horrible and agonizing execution, and we know that many of his followers across the centuries have given their lives in his service. Again the late twentieth century is no exception.

There continue to be Christians throughout the world whose discipleship exacts a high price as they face the harsh reality of injustice and oppression. Their stories come to us with disturbing regularity: a Roman Catholic archbishop slain at the altar of his church in El Salvador, in the very act of celebrating the Mass; a Methodist bishop in Bolivia, imprisoned, interrogated, and exiled; church leaders in South Africa wrestling with a legacy of racial oppression as they seek integrity in their Christian witness; and in the United States, behind the prophets of the Sixties, the many thousands whose witness, often at the cost of imprisonment, physical abuse, and even their very lives, brought their nation to a new understanding of its heritage of liberty and justice for all.

THE DILEMMA OF DISCIPLESHIP

For those of us in "first world" countries such as the United States, all of this presents a very real dilemma. We try to maintain a faithful witness in our life and work, but we are acutely aware that our Christian discipleship is rarely very costly and is much less dramatic. We live our lives in the subtle grip of technological affluence, even when our share of it is quite modest. The challenges we face are more likely to be those of single parenting, overeating, teenage drug abuse, video addiction, unemployment, and professional competition. We are so consumed with meeting the daily struggle to survive the pressures of this affluence that we seem to have no energy—physically, emotionally, intellectually, or spiritually—to become involved with the struggles of the martyrs in our own country, never mind anywhere else.

Nor does it help to have our problems repeatedly diagnosed by sociologists, psychologists, or pulpiteers. Those of us who are overweight are rarely encouraged by reminders that every two seconds a human being somewhere in the world dies of starvation. Those of us who are parents of teenage sons and daughters, the next in line to inherit our world, are unlikely to be heartened by the reminder that nuclear war is still a lethal possibility. Deep down we know that we should join either with those Christians who protest against the arms race or with those who affirm it as the surest balance of international power. We know that to take no position at all is the height of irresponsibility, yet that is exactly what most of us find ourselves doing. Those of us facing broken marriages, with bitter disputes over property and child custody, are seldom in the mood to hear arguments on the one hand for the liberation of women from male-dominated relationships or on the other hand for the family as a Christian institution to be maintained at all costs.

This is not to say that such analyses and exhortations are irrelevant. On the contrary, they have often proved to be the cutting edge of Christian discipleship in our time, reminding us that the gospel impacts human relationships and social structures at every level of our existence. But for most of us, the problems are at once more mundane and more immediate. Faced with such daily pressures at home and at work, our response to the larger vision of discipleship for the most part tends to be one of exasperation: "What can *I* do about the problems of the world? *How* can I do anything?"

THE ANGUISH OF DISCIPLESHIP

These are not empty questions. Most of us ask them with sincerity, at times with anguish, and we would very much like to have them answered. It is not that the challenge of discipleship impels us to a pessimistic view of the world. Much around us affirms the coming reign of God, not least the dramatic breakthrough in political freedoms with which the final decade of the century has been ushered in. But once we are called to discipleship, we begin to see the enormity of the task that still remains. However sure the final victory of Christ might be, as long as even one child is hungry, as long as even one human being suffers from injustice, there can be no rest for the Christian disciple.

In spite of the strides being made against oppression across the world, we continue to be moved by the photographs of starving children staring at us with empty eyes and enlarged stomachs. We continue to be sickened by the stark remnants of the holocausts in our time—the mass graves, the torture chambers, and the concentration camps. We continue to view the terrible cost of human conflict—the bombings in Northern Ireland and Lebanon, the ragged stumps where once there were healthy limbs on the people of Afghanistan and Nicaragua, and the chilling reminder that Middle East nations with strong cultural and religious ties can still engage in mutual genocide and threaten global war. While in the United States, the unbridled greed in high finance which superciliously plays games with the fruits of ordinary people's hard work, the dishonesty in government which masquerades as patriotism, and the widespread use of drugs, illicit and otherwise, all continue to wreak social, ethical, and family havoc.

But this is not all. As we see the continued evidence in the world of human rebellion against God, we find ourselves to be part of it. The commandment of Jesus was clear: We should love God and love our neighbors as ourselves. Yet we find ourselves wondering whether we will ever be able to obey this command.

"They will know we are Christians by our love," runs the well-known refrain. Well, on a good day, maybe; but on most days it would be difficult to tell. And, with a harsh irony, Sundays seem to test us most of all. As we scramble to get to church, we glance across the street to our neighborly pagan, who is leisurely sniffing the morning before relaxing with the Sunday paper and a second cup of coffee; and we might be forgiven for a moment of real doubt. Surely *we* are the ones who are supposed to have the love and the peace of God!

THE SEARCH FOR GOD'S WILL

We are indeed searching for answers, searching for God's will in our lives, and for some assurance that in the midst of the tension in which we live, we are following the carpenter from Nazareth. Our ethnic brothers and sisters in the church—Hispanic, Black, Native American, Asian—as well as our sisters and brothers throughout the world, remind us that God's salvation is a new order of justice as well as love. They gently but firmly rebuke us for our churchly self-centeredness and our abuse of the gospel as a spiritual analgesic or amphetamine.

We hear their word, and it cuts us to the quick. We badly need to know how we can play our part in congregations that are no longer local but global. We need to be convinced that our witness in these places of worship and fellowship has a degree of integrity and that our community outreach has some relevance to the gospel.

The word we used earlier, *anguish*, is not too strong at all. Once we hear the call to discipleship, once we begin to sense the ongoing task of Jesus Christ to redeem the human race from its sin and suffering, and once we begin to see the extent of God's concern for our planet, there is no other way to describe what we feel. We are deeply, deeply anguished.

THE POWER OF DISCIPLESHIP

All of this sends us with renewed urgency back to the scriptures, where we are heartened to find that this anguish is not new. As Paul makes clear in his letter to the church at Rome, it is as old as human sin. For when we come to the Word of God with the hunger of disciples seeking to serve Jesus Christ, the dynamics of our salvation strike us with a new and critical self-awareness.

First comes a deeper repentance, as we realize the true extent of our captivity to sin:

> I do not understand my own actions. For I do not do what I want, but I do the very thing I hate. Now if I do what I do not want, I agree that the law is good. But in fact it is no longer I that do it, but sin that dwells within me. For I know that nothing good dwells within me, that is, in my flesh. I can will what is right, but I cannot do it. For I do not do the good I want, but the evil I do not want is what I do. . . . For I delight in the law of God in my inmost self, but I see in my members another law at war with the law of my mind, making me captive to the law of sin that dwells in my members. Wretched man that I am! Who will rescue me from this body of death? (Rom. 7:15-19, 22-24).

Then comes a new sense of release, as we experience more profoundly the depths of our forgiveness and reconciliation in Christ:

> There is therefore now no condemnation for those who are in Christ Jesus. For the law of the Spirit of life in Christ Jesus has

set you free from the law of sin and of death. For God has done what the law, weakened by the flesh, could not do: by sending his own Son in the likeness of sinful flesh, and to deal with sin, he condemned sin in the flesh, so that the just requirement of the law might be fulfilled in us, who walk not according to the flesh but according to the Spirit. . . . For all who are led by the Spirit of God are children of God. For you did not receive a spirit of slavery to fall back into fear, but you have received a spirit of adoption. When we cry, "Abba! Father!" it is that very Spirit bearing witness with our spirit that we are children of God, and if children, the heirs, heirs of God and joint heirs with Christ (Rom. 8:1-4, 14-17a).

Theologians refer to this great truth as the doctrine of justification by faith, and it has been the taproot of Protestantism ever since the Reformation. It is the declaration by God in Christ that in spite of our sin, in spite of our imperfections, *we are accepted by God just as we are—warts and all.* And more, it is the assurance that when we do the best we can to follow Jesus Christ, that too is good enough for God.

We are no longer measured by what we know we ought to do, nor yet by what others do; still less by what others tell us we ought to do. We are free from all such burdens because we know that we are reconciled as members of God's family. Whatever the level of our accomplishment—and significantly, whatever the level of our commitment also—we have the deep joy and peace of knowing that we are once again in tune with the things of eternity.

The words of the old hymn are profound, and we should sing them thoughtfully:

> 'Twas grace that taught my heart to fear,
> And grace my fears relieved:
> How precious did that grace appear
> The hour I first believed.[1]

Just as the inviting power of grace awakens us to the reality of our separation from God, the reconciling power of grace restores us to God's love. We know this because the carpenter from Nazareth promised it. And his promise holds true because God raised him from the dead.

All of this we see with the more penetrating illumination of Christian discipleship, once we have made the commitment to follow Jesus Christ in deed as well as word. For once we have accepted the condition of unconditional obedience to Christ, we in turn are honored by the Holy Spirit with profound new insights into the work of God in the world.

THE OBLIGATIONS OF DISCIPLESHIP

In other words, having made this commitment to Christ, we are trusted with more information about the purpose of our call and with more responsibility for the task in hand. Thus it was with the first disciples, to whom Jesus appeared after his resurrection. Not only did he assure them of his victory over sin and death, but he also commissioned them for the work that lay ahead.

That commission comes to us today with the same challenge and the same promise. Jesus challenges us to become his disciples in preparing for God's salvation of the world, and he promises us the privilege of his friendship. Moreover, this is the offer of a true friendship—a sharing of *everything*.

This sharing of everything, however, works both ways. Not only are we entrusted with deeper insights into our sin and salvation, but we are also expected to join Christ more directly and sympathetically in the suffering and injustice of the world.

As Paul goes on to say in Romans, we are heirs with Christ provided we suffer with him in order that we might be glorified with him. Christ's victory over sin is not yet here in its fullness, and those who accept his call to discipleship must be ready for a struggle, not only with their own residual resistance to God's grace, but also with the resistance of a sinful world:

I consider that the sufferings of this present time are not worth comparing with the glory about to be revealed to us. For the creation waits with eager longing for the revealing of the children of God; . . . in hope that the creation itself will be set free from its bondage to decay and will obtain the freedom of the glory of the children of God. We know that the whole creation has been groaning in labor pains until now; and not only the creation, but we ourselves, who have the first fruits of the Spirit, groan inwardly while we wait for adoption, the redemption of our bodies. For in hope we were saved. Now hope that is seen is not hope. For who hopes for what is seen?

But if we hope for what we do not see, we wait for it with patience (Rom. 8:18-19, 21-25).

THE WORLDLY SUFFERING OF DISCIPLESHIP

The message is at once exhilarating and sobering. However joyfully we might be reconciled to God as sons and daughters, however liberating it is to be accepted by God, our imperfections notwithstanding, there is a larger context for our discipleship. God's plan of salvation has global, indeed cosmic dimensions. Just as we have been given new life through our reconciliation with God in Christ, so God intends new life for the whole of creation. Just as our own rebirth comes through the labor and suffering of Jesus Christ, so does that of the world. As disciples of Jesus Christ we are called to share in that labor and suffering.

We have found personal forgiveness and reconciliation in Christ, as have countless others. But now our call to discipleship sends us back into the world where we are confronted very directly with the realities of sin, suffering, and evil, which make our personal sin pale by comparison. For now we see that sin and suffering are not just personal but global and systemic. Now we are much more aware of the injustice of oppression, the torment of disease, the scandal of starvation, and the cheapness of human life.

In other words, the joy and the freedom of personal discipleship lead us inexorably to the challenge of global discipleship. And the question that now presses us is, How can we be obedient to Jesus Christ in a world that remains rebellious against God, not least because we still find rebellious tendencies in ourselves?

THE PITFALL OF SPIRITUAL WITHDRAWAL

Needless to say, it is possible to avoid this challenge of the task by effecting a spiritual withdrawal from the world—a withdrawal made all the more tempting by the deepened knowledge of God which continues to result from our commitment to an intentional walk with Christ and a disciplined communion with the Holy Spirit. The privilege of spiritual oneness with Christ makes us yearn for even more—just as the disciples were unwilling to leave the Mount of Transfiguration (Matt. 17:4; Mark 9:5). We hunger and thirst for the living Word with an intensity we never before thought possible, and we resent the interference of worldly concerns and duties that seem to distract us from such spiritual pursuits.

To go down this road, however, is little short of tragic, because there is no quicker way to compromise our discipleship and blur our spiritual perspectives. When we seek communion with God at the expense of worldly living, whether we do so in the safety of churchly surroundings or in the aloofness of a pious disdain for the world, we begin to look around us with a jaundiced eye. We not only forget that God's grace still has much to accomplish in our own lives. What is far more important, we lose sight of the worldly imperative of the gospel: that this is the planet which, with all its sin and evil, Jesus came to save. In the words of the Scottish poet, Edwin Muir, we take the Word made flesh and make it word again.[2]

By contrast, those disciples who work through the challenge of their task come to see, along with the Christ whom they serve, that God will indeed go out to look for the lost sheep rather than stay with the ninety and nine in the fold. They come to grasp the true meaning of the parable in which the feast is given for the returned prodigal, not the son who stayed at home. They grow in their understanding that the criterion for living in the kingdom of God is not right belief, but right action (Matt. 25:31-46; James 1:22-25, 2:14-26). Most important of all, the full weight of the gospel emerges for them with clarity and with force: *that the world is God's sphere of salvation, and disciples of the Savior must join him where he is at work.*

THE HOPE OF DISCIPLESHIP

There are those, of course, who argue that a discipleship patterned too strictly on the life and teaching of Jesus is unrealistic. Paul is right, their argument goes. The world is indeed waiting for a rebirth. But it won't happen this side of eternity, and in the meantime the world remains as imperfect as ever it was. We must therefore learn to live with these imperfections, trusting God to forgive us for the compromises we have to make. After all, not much can be done about the evil and suffering we see around us. The best we can do is to follow Christ faithfully in our daily lives and trust God to deal in due time with these larger problems.

Even a cursory reading of scripture, however, indicates that this view of Christian discipleship falls far short of the New Testament vision of God's salvation. Paul's message is one of hope—hope for the world as one day it will be and hope for the new age announced and inaugurated by Jesus Christ. Those of us called to follow this Savior must not only share his vision of the new age, but share it *to the fullest*.

That is why the call to discipleship comes with such a strong word of warning. Jesus was nothing if not honest. If we accept the identity of being his disciples, we must be ready to share in his sufferings as well as in his victory. To answer the call means nothing less than patterning ourselves after Jesus in every aspect of our existence. Mistakes there will be, and shortcomings. But there must be no compromise of *intent*. We must be ready to give all in his service, if need be, to the laying down of our lives.

AN IMPOSSIBLE TENSION?

At this point, many of us become apprehensive. Is discipleship such a radical alternative that we must live in an impossible tension? Do the realities of a faithful Christian witness cancel out the freedom of our new relationship with God by taking us back to the dilemma of Romans 7—knowing what we ought to be doing in the world, but finding ourselves unable to do it? Is the only way to faithful discipleship the way of the martyr, taking Christ's words literally, giving away all that we have in order to feed the poor and following him to the cross? As we have noted, some Christians in our day and age make precisely that witness. They show us that it is indeed possible to sell everything we have for the poor and to live simply in the midst of affluence. Should we not be doing likewise?

As with the challenge of our call, the answer once again lies with God's grace. Christ does not ask more of us as his disciples in the world than we are able to accomplish in the love and power of the Holy Spirit. With the call to discipleship comes the promise of grace to sustain us in the journey that lies ahead, wherever it may lead, and whatever task it may require of us:

> Through many dangers, toils, and snares,
> I have already come;
> 'Tis grace hath brought me safe thus far,
> And grace will lead me home.[3]

On my kitchen wall is a plaque given to me many years ago by a woman who knew the truth of what it says: "The will of God will never lead you where the grace of God cannot keep you." God has not forgiven us our sins and weaknesses in order to lay fresh failures on us. Christ does not ask of us anything we are not able to carry out in the strength of his Spirit. "Thanks be to God," said Paul, "through Jesus Christ our Lord. . . . You are not in the flesh; you are in the Spirit, since the Spirit of God dwells in you" (Rom. 7:25, 8:9).

THE TASK OF DISCIPLESHIP

The whole point about discipleship is that we need not worry about what Christ *might* ask us to do. The question rather to be asked is, What does Christ want us to do *right now?* For whatever Christ asks us to do will always be accompanied by two clear assurances from the Holy Spirit: We will know that it is unquestionably the right thing to do at the time; and we will be given whatever strength and purpose we need at the time to accomplish it. Whenever we find ourselves worrying about what we might need to do for Christ at some point, or about whether we will be able to meet the challenge of joining the saints and martyrs of the church as faithful disciples, it is almost always a sign that we are evading a more obvious and probably quite simple task that Christ needs doing here and now; and that we should be getting on with it.

THE CONDITION OF DISCIPLESHIP

There is, however, an important proviso to all of this; and as we might expect, given our residual sinful resistance to God's grace, it lies within ourselves. Yes, God will sustain us in whatever we are called to do. And yes, nothing in the whole creation, even a creation in the birthpangs of new life, can separate us from the love and power of that grace—nothing, that is, save our freedom to accept or reject God's call. For the grace of God is so gracious that we are always given the choice of accepting or rejecting our discipleship—which is what ultimately makes our discipleship costly. Paul reminds us of it over and over again in Romans 8: *If the Spirit* of God is with us; *if* we join with Christ in his suffering; *if* we are children of God; *if* we hope for what we do not see; *if.* . . . Later in the epistle, Paul makes the point even more forcefully:

> I appeal to you, therefore, brothers and sisters, by the mercies of God, to present your bodies as a living sacrifice, holy and acceptable to God, which is your spiritual worship. Do not be conformed to this world, but be transformed by the renewing of your minds, so that you may discern what is the will of God—what is good and acceptable and perfect (Rom. 12:1-2).

This is not an appeal, we should note, to exercise a self-discipline, or an exhortation to strive for global transformation. The advice is at once simple and more profound: Allow God's grace to work in our lives. For the grace of God is the only strength in which we can be faithful disciples.

THE OBEDIENCE OF DISCIPLESHIP

The key word in all of this is *obedience*, a word that is deeply principled, yet deeply relational. The fundamental question for the Christian disciple must always be, "How do I know that I am obedient? How do I know that what I am doing is the will of God?" Paul's answer is once again to affirm the grace of God:

> Likewise the Spirit helps us in our weakness; . . . that very Spirit intercedes with sighs too deep for words. And God, who searches the heart, knows what is the mind of the Spirit, because the Spirit intercedes for the saints according to the will of God. We know that all things work together for good for those who love God, who are called according to his purpose (Rom. 8:26-28).

In other words, Christians who accept the grace of God, who permit the strength and the power and the love and the peace of God to work in their lives, have the assurance of an obedient discipleship. Theirs will not be a perfect discipleship, but it will be the best they can offer, and it will be wholly acceptable to God.

Christians who endeavor to be disciples *without* this grace, however, will lack the capacity for obedience and will find themselves still caught in the dilemma of knowing what ought to be done, but never being able to do it. Such Christians never have peace of mind. They are filled with constant uncertainty and are persistently stung by the witness of those whose discipleship is more costly.

A DEEP UNEASE

If we can accept the word of countless clergy and laity across the land, this is where a sizeable number of North American Christians find themselves today. They are constantly trying to do the best they can in the ambivalences of the world in which they live and work, but they are never sure that their best is good enough for God. They are willing and ready to make a commitment to a reliable and faithful discipleship, for they know deep down that this is what they need to do. If there is a quality common to most American churchgoers, it is sound common sense. They have rightly become suspicious of contemporary forms of spirituality that extol the development of human personhood to the neglect of God's work in the world. They are equally mistrustful of exhortations to a worldly involvement that seem to render the grace of God peripheral to the task in hand. They know that discipleship is more, much more than this, and they are ready, as the saying goes, to quit cutting bait and to start fishing.

BACK TO OUR ROOTS

In the mid-1980s, the answer to these questions emerged with some cogency. The occasion was the Bicentennial of American Methodism, to be followed before the end of the decade by the 250th anniversaries of John Wesley's Aldersgate Street experience, May 24, 1738, and his venture into open-air preaching, April 2, 1739. These celebrations prompted Methodists the world over to go back to their roots; and in so doing, the faithful discipleship of their eighteenth-century forebears spoke loud and clear to this latest generation of "methodical" Christians. They found that the answer to the anguish and dilemma of their discipleship lay in some very simple and basic ways of living out their witness in the world.

THE PRACTICE OF DISCIPLESHIP

We learned from our early mentors that faithful discipleship lies not only in repentance, forgiveness, and reconciliation, but also in certain well-tried practices through which Christians across the centuries have opened themselves to God's grace. We found that John Wesley had defined these disciplines as *works of mercy* and *works of piety*, and had instilled in the early Methodists the necessity of practicing them regularly and, just as important, of holding them in balance.

A RING OF COMMON SENSE

Moreover, we found that "methodical" discipleship, while projecting a somewhat routine approach to the Christian life, had a ring of sound common sense. It fell like music on the ears of faithful church members who had suffered, and continue to suffer, a cacophany of conflicting demands on their time and energies, most of which seem designed more to bolster the confidence of hesitant church leadership than to equip the servants of Jesus Christ for their task in the world.

The reasoning of the early Methodists is quite easy to follow. If the call of Christ to discipleship does make requirements of us; if these requirements are clearly laid out in the teachings of Jesus; if they can be met only by availing ourselves of God's grace—something which is clear to any Christian who has tried to meet them in his or her own strength alone; and if the church has found across the centuries that there are certain reliable channels for this grace; then good sense must surely dictate that Christians use these means of grace in the fullest possible way in order to fulfill their obligations to Jesus Christ.

By the same token, if Christians are not using these means of grace, are not meeting their obligations to Jesus Christ in the world, and as a result are finding their discipleship fraught with ambivalence and uncertainty, then we should be asking ourselves with some urgency why we are not doing something about it.

A PRACTICAL EXAMPLE

The early Methodists faced the same kinds of problems, and their solutions, as we might expect, were practical and down-to-earth. The genius of their approach came home to me many years ago when I was a student at Oxford University. Like most new students, I arrived with all sorts of good resolutions to make the best of my time and opportunities. Moreover, having been brought up as a Methodist, perhaps more than most I was resolved to be "methodical," being very aware that this had been Wesley's place of study more than 200 years earlier.

One of my resolutions was that I was going to keep physically fit, and I decided that a good way to do this would be to go for a run each morning before breakfast. The first week, I ran every morning. Breakfast took on new meaning, and I felt invigorated and refreshed for the day's work. The second week, I missed a couple of mornings. The third week, I missed all but one morning. The fourth week I missed altogether, and the fifth week I made an amended resolution—that *next* year I would go running each morning!

The following year, however, I took a precautionary measure. I asked the person next door if he would like to go running with me. "Good idea," he said; and with somewhat mixed feelings, I knew I was committed. On the days I was late, he would bang on my door with a cheery word, "Time to be going!" There were several mornings, by no means as many, when I would return the favor. Occasionally, we would both be late, insisting that we were just about to come and get the other. But we made it all through the year, every morning.

MUTUAL HELP AND SUPPORT

There is no need to explore this as a phenomenon of the human will. It merely illustrates that some things are done better by two people than by one. We find it in every walk of life. Meals tend to be better planned and cooked when there is more than one person at the table. Construction engineers on a building site find a workmate indispensable. Airline pilots doing a preflight check rely on each other's memory. Sanitary engineers collecting garbage need a team to drive and pick up at the same time. Mountaineers roped together for a climb, athletes pacing one another for a race, all need the help and support of others. In short, anything that is subject to human limitation or error requires the collegial presence of another person to ensure reliability. It is a fact of life.

Yet as Christians, we persistently neglect to apply this principle to the basics of our discipleship. We prefer to keep our options open, to "remain flexible," and to go in whichever direction seems desirable or appropriate or convenient—anything, in fact, but to follow the guidelines Jesus gave us for being his disciples. Little wonder, then that we find ourselves constantly searching for the meaning of our Christian commitment, yet seeking the easy way, the shortcut, the quick fix, or the latest formula for guaranteed instant churchly success. By failing to help one another to be open to God's grace, we are deliberately opting for self-sufficiency in our discipleship. And that, as we have clearly seen in scripture, is a contradiction in terms. To use Wesley's vivid language, it means that we are making shipwreck of our faith.

THE NEED FOR LEADERS

This self-sufficient approach to discipleship in our time has engendered a climate in which the desire to serve people far outweighs the need to challenge them; so much so, that a call to accountability is often rejected as impracticable. The early Methodists, by contrast, understood the need for mentors in discipleship. They were aware of the importance of role models who led by example. In many congregations today, however, going to church has come to be perceived as well-nigh incompatible with costly discipleship, so that leaders who challenge by their example have little if any role to play. H. Richard Niebuhr's famous *dictum* is turned inside out. Instead of the gospel comforting the afflicted and afflicting the comfortable, it pampers the comfortable to the neglect of the afflicted—and for no other reason than that the alternative seems to be impossibly unrealistic. What is needed is some practical format for the exercise of costly discipleship *within* the average American congregation, so that leadership by example might once again impact the life and work of the church.

A PATTERN FOR DISCIPLESHIP

There are United Methodists who have believed for some time—
and are now even more convinced—that our heritage in Wesley's
early Methodist societies provides us with just such a model: the
class meeting. Nor is it mere coincidence that informed colleagues
from other denominations regularly point out to us that this is the
genius of Methodism.

The class meeting was a weekly gathering, a subdivision of the
early societies, at which members were required to give an account
to one another of their discipleship and thereby to sustain each
other in their witness. These meetings were regarded by Wesley as
the "sinews" of the Methodist movement, the means by which
members "watched over one another in love."[4] They were
grounded in solid theological principles which could readily be
grasped, making them not only a point of mutual accountability,
but also a rich source of the gospel tradition.

Week by week, the early Methodists helped each other plumb
the depths of the scriptures and the teachings of the church; and it
showed in their discipleship—how it showed. They followed Jesus
of Nazareth with integrity. They accepted his guidelines for doing
the work of God in the world, endeavored to follow them faithfully
in their daily living, and all the while availed themselves regularly
of the means of grace.

It's high time we take the necessary steps to follow their example
and drink deeply, as they did, from the well of the gospel, when
many shallow ponds are offering mere reflections of the Word. We
don't need renewal in our congregations. We merely need to exercise some basic common sense.

For Thought and Discussion

1. What does it mean to you when you pray, "Thy kingdom come, thy will be done on earth as it is in heaven"?

2. Has your Christian discipleship proved costly? Rewarding?

3. How should Christians in an affluent culture respond to the witness of costly discipleship in the midst of poverty or oppression?

4. Has the dilemma expressed by Paul in Romans 7 been resolved in your life?

5. Discuss the statement on page 10, "that the world is God's sphere of salvation, and disciples of the Savior must join him where he is at work."

6. "Mistakes there will be, and shortcomings. But there must be no compromise of *intent*" (page 11). Discuss.

7. "The will of God will never lead you where the grace of God cannot keep you" (page 12). Has this been true in your Christian life?

8. Do you agree that "methodical" discipleship is a matter of "common sense"?

Chapter 2

Early Methodist Discipleship

THE WESLEY BROTHERS

There are millions of Christians today who call themselves Methodists. They belong to more than a hundred denominations; they are to be found in almost every country of the world; and they are very diverse in their cultural and theological expressions of the gospel. Yet they all trace their lineage back to two Anglican clergymen of the eighteenth century, who happened also to be brothers: John and Charles Wesley.

While both brothers were instrumental in founding the Methodist movement, Charles became known primarily for his hymns. Hundreds of them are still sung by Methodists, and some of them have been claimed by the world church. Favorites such as "Hark! the Herald Angels Sing," "Christ the Lord Is Risen Today," and "Jesus, Lover of My Soul" rank with the best liturgical language of the Christian tradition. Indeed, largely because of Charles' poetic genius, Methodism is said to have been "born in song." To this day, well-worn copies of hymnals survive as family heirlooms, indicating that they were carried to worship and midweek meetings along with Bibles, and were just as much used.

It was John Wesley, however, who emerged as the spiritual leader of the early Methodist movement. Not only did he prove to have considerable skills as an organizer, but his training and background made him especially equipped to forge a practical understanding of what it meant to be a Christian in the world. He was gifted with the spiritual power of discipleship, but he applied it through some very simple, down-to-earth principles from which we still have a great deal to learn.

WESLEY THE THEOLOGIAN

To understand John Wesley's leadership of early Methodism, we must turn first to his theology. This task is rendered at once easy

21

and difficult by the nature of his ministry. On the one hand, his journal and his letters give us perhaps the most complete record of any church leader's life and work, helping us to know him as a human being with limitations as well as strengths. On the other hand, precisely because this detailed record is so fascinating, it is easy to overlook the theological foundations on which he based his very active ministry. So much about his organization of the Methodist societies marks him as a brilliant organizer that his accomplishments as a theologian are only now being acknowledged.

The first thing we must note is that his theology is very straightforward and down to earth, and for a good reason. John Wesley was an evangelist, and true evangelists are always in touch with the world—something which can prove disconcerting to those of us who live our lives within the safety of church walls. He was out and about most of the time, " 'going into the highways and hedges,' which none else will do." [5] As he did so, he confronted people with the gospel, often challenging their way of life quite directly, yet always imparting to them the love of God in Jesus Christ.

The result was that Wesley developed a rapport with ordinary men and women. He understood their feelings, their needs, and their language; and in many ways he became one oft them. As Albert Outler put it, Wesley was not "a theologian's theologian. His chief intellectual interest, and achievement, was in what one could call a folk theology: the Christian message in its fullness and integrity, in 'plain words for plain people.' " [6]

THE TENSION OF THE GOSPEL

This concern to make theology relevant for common folk means that Wesley did not have the time, and probably not the inclination, to put together a detailed exposition of the Christian faith. Yet his writings, when read in the context of his evangelistic outreach, express with remarkable clarity the essential tension of the Christian faith: the vision of the gospel over against the reality of worldly living.

Wesley came to understand this tension as he exercised his ministry among ordinary, humble Christians, who were doing their best to live out their faith in the world. Indeed, it is this understanding that arguably makes him the most significant church leader in the whole of Protestantism. He found that the faith of simple people had as much integrity as the teachings of the church, so he took seriously their reaction to the message he and his preachers proclaimed. At the same time, however, he granted full authority to the laws and doctrines of the Church of England and was critical of those who would not affirm or practice them. He looked upon the church with great affection as "the mother of us all."[7]

WESLEY'S UPBRINGING

All of this was due in no small measure to the influence of his parents, both of whom had converted to the Church of England from Nonconformist backgrounds, in this case Presbyterian. With the dedication of those who have taken such a step, they instilled in their children the importance of the church as a visible institution. In the church were to be found right teaching and the time-honored disciples of the Christian life. To ignore these, or to try to improve on them unnecessarily, was not only a waste of time, as Wesley saw it; it was also to risk repeating the errors of the past. Even worse, to spend so much time on things which had already been agreed was bound to divert attention from the more important tasks of Christian discipleship.

AN INFLUENTIAL MOTHER

Yet Wesley was not the typical Church of England clergyman of his day. He had begun at an early age to pursue a personal spiritual life which quickly set him apart from most of his clerical contemporaries. This again was due in no small measure to parental influence, and in particular that of his mother, Susanna Wesley.

By all accounts, this was a remarkable woman. She regarded the development of the spiritual life of her children as no less important than their emotional and physical well-being, and saw to it that they were intentionally nurtured in this regard. While they were growing up in the rectory at Epworth, she set aside an evening each week for each child—John's evening was Thursday—in order to instruct them in the things of God.

The habits they thus acquired at this formative stage in their lives were to prove long-lasting. Certainly the correspondence John exchanged with his mother when he was a student at Oxford University is eloquent testimony to her influence.[8] And when his brother Charles and some fellow students drew on John's leadership for their small devotional groups at Oxford, known as the Holy Club, their methodical approach to spiritual disciplines and practical good works bore clear signs of the sound training of their mother. It also earned them the nickname "Methodist," by which the movement as a whole became known in due course, even though Wesley himself never liked it.

WESLEY'S CHURCHMANSHIP

Wesley's churchmanship was derived not only from the Church of England, however, but also from the rich tapestry of the broader English Protestant heritage. As an Anglican, he affirmed the authority and tradition of the visible church. But he was also influenced by the Puritan concept of the "gathered church"—particular communities of faith brought together by the Holy Spirit and grounded on the authority of scripture alone.

Wesley emphasized both concepts. He acknowledged the validity of a gathered community, elected by God for a purpose; but this did not negate the wider concept of an inclusive and visible church, reaching out to all, firmly in and of the world, a means of God's prevenient grace.

ECCLESIOLA IN ECCLESIA

The phrase that best describes this twofold view of the church came out of seventeenth-century German pietism: *ecclesiola in ecclesia*, or "little church" in the "big church." Wesley found that the *ecclesiola*, the little church, was a self-evident reality among the people to whom he ministered in the Methodist societies. Clearly these groups had been gathered together by God, and blessed with power and purpose. Yet Wesley believed it was important to keep them firmly within the visible Church of England, grounded in the mainstream of the Christian tradition. As long as he lived, he regarded these *ecclesiolae* as valid only insofar as they were part of the larger church, the *ecclesia*.

REFORM OF THE CHURCH

As Frank Baker has shown in great detail, Wesley's avowed purpose was not to form a new church, but to reform the old one;[9] and in spite of many pressures to separate, this remained the purpose of his ministry. As we know, his purpose was thwarted: partly by a stubborn Church of England, which refused to acknowledge the potential of Methodist societies to revitalize the church, but also by the events of political history, which made it necessary to give his blessing to the formation of a Methodist church in North America. Yet, to the end of his life, Wesley resisted separation of the English societies from the Church of England as an unnecessary schism. His emphasis was on discipleship *within* the church, not disciplinary or doctrinal disputes that might divide it.

REACHING OUT TO ALL

Even so, the very nature of the Methodist societies as "little churches" was bound to create an inherent separatist tendency in the movement. Paradoxically, the chief reason for this was Wesley's own insistence that the purpose of the church be given priority over its function. This was the true meaning of discipleship as he saw it—the *working out* of salvation. As the early Methodists took up this task and became living witnesses to their faith, church order and doctrine became less important to Wesley than reaching out to "the tinners in Cornwall, the keelmen in Newcastle, the colliers in Kingswood and Staffordshire, the drunkards, the swearers, the Sabbath-breakers of Moorfield, and the harlots of Drury Lane."[10]

THE WORLD HIS PARISH

The more he reached out, the more he was banned from the pulpits of Anglican parishes. But this did not deter him, for his commission was clear:

> God in Scripture commands me, according to my power, to instruct the ignorant, reform the wicked, confirm the virtuous.

Man forbids me to do this in another's parish: that is, in effect, to do it at all; seeing I have no parish of my own, nor probably ever shall. Whom, then, shall I hear, God or man? . . . *I look upon all the world as my parish;* this far I mean, that in whatever part of it I am, I judge it meet, right, and my bounden duty to declare unto all that are willing to hear the glad tidings of salvation. This is the work which I know God has called me to do. And sure I am that his blessing attends it.[11]

CHURCHLY TENSIONS

Wesley was aware that going into the fields with the gospel would be a source of tension with the Church of England. Indeed, as the Methodist movement gathered momentum, separation from the Church of England in many ways seemed the most obvious step to take. Anglican critics gave every indication that they regarded the societies as a divisive movement, and would probably have been happy to see them as a separated body.

But on this point, Wesley's theology always checked the pragmatism of his polity. He firmly believed that the spirit of Methodism would be seriously hindered by separation from the mother church. Arguing strongly for the legitimacy of the Methodist societies *within* Anglican faith and practice, he answered his critics by pointing out that the purpose of the societies was to encourage members to strengthen each other by talking and praying together as often as possible. Not only was this wholly in keeping with the disciplines of the church, it was also "grounded on the plainest reason, and on so many scriptures both of the Old Testament and New, that it would be tedious to recite them."[12]

AGAINST SCHISM

The problem was that many of the rank-and-file Methodists did not see things this way. It was possible during the eighteenth century to obtain a license quite readily as a "dissenting congregation," which gave the right to hold regular Sunday worship services and to have an independent church organization. It seemed unreasonable to many of the Methodists, therefore, that they should have to remain part of the Church of England.

Wesley accordingly took pains to warn the members of the societies against the ill effects of breaking away from the church. The aims of separation, he maintained, were invariably thwarted by the means. "The experiment has been so frequently tried already, and the success has never answered the expectation."[13] Should this occur in Methodism, he noted as late as 1789, the result would be the dwindling of those who separated into "a dull, dry party." And this, he declared, he would do all in his power to prevent as long as he lived. The essence of his argument was forceful: Separation, if avoidable, was a serious distraction from the priorities of the faith.

In his sermon, "On Schism," Wesley defined such a step as inherently evil, a grievous breach of the law of love, and contrary to the nature of the faith that ought to unite Christians. Schism, being evil in itself, provided evil fruits, and opened a door to uncharitable judgments, which in turn led to slandering and backbiting. These were not imaginary results, said Wesley, but plain facts, borne out by events in his own experience. The question was not separation *per se*. Clearly if a church should lead members against the scriptures or into some other false teaching, then they should separate. The sin was *unnecessary* division.[14]

Wesley upheld this position consistently. It caused more than a few broken relationships with his preachers, and it was never appreciated by the hierarchy of the Church of England. But in the spirit and the structure of *ecclesiola in ecclesia*, he saw that authentic discipleship implied not only freedom, but also accountability, and that each should be given equal emphasis. The Methodist societies were no mere expedient. They were based on a sound and sensitive understanding of the church as the wellspring of faithful Christian living.

FORMATIVE FACTORS

The church of England did not, however, provide the spiritual dynamic of early Methodism. This came from two other formative factors in Wesley's churchmanship, both of them expressions of *ecclesiola in ecclesia*.

The Religious Societies

The first of these was the *religious societies*, which appeared in England during the latter part of the seventeenth century. They were organized through the influence of Anthony Horneck, a Lutheran minister who had settled in England. Horneck had been familiar with the *collegia pietatis* of German pietism—small house groups that met under the leadership of Jakob Philipp Spener, first in Frankfurt and then elsewhere in Germany. Their aim was to develop a more disciplined spiritual life for their members, which the established Lutheran church was not providing. When groups of young men in London indicated similar interests, Horneck drew up a set of rules for them—though he was careful to stipulate that they were to "keep close" to the Church of England in all of their affairs.

As the societies spread through London and other parts of the country, they coordinated their work through the Society for Promoting Christian Knowledge (SPCK), founded in 1699, and the Society for the Propagation of the Gospel in Foreign Parts (SPG), founded in 1701. Wesley became a corresponding member of the SPCK in August 1732; though he was probably familiar with the format of the societies from his boyhood days. His father, Samuel Wesley, had founded one at Epworth in 1701; and Susanna Wesley had also used the model, somewhat adapted, when she began to hold what she called "enlarged family prayers" in the Epworth rectory in 1712—a good way of circumventing the rules of the Societies, which restricted membership to men only.

Lay leadership was a mark of these societies from the very beginning. Two "stewards" were appointed to guide the spiritual discussion of the meetings, in which liturgy and music also played a role. Members were encouraged to speak openly to one another and to share what was on their hearts in ways that were not possible in other contexts.[15]

The Societies also promoted the practical aspects of Christian discipleship. By the turn of the eighteenth century, they had become increasingly involved in caring for the poor, relieving debt, visiting the sick, providing for orphans, and setting up more than a hundred schools in London and the suburbs.

Although in decline when Methodism took shape in the mid-eighteenth century, the Religious Societies had by no means disappeared; and in many ways they provided direct precedents for the Methodist movement. In addition to the two aspects of their work we have mentioned—the role of lay leadership and the involvement in direct social outreach—they also provided an immediate context for the Methodist revival. In the first place, they were receptive to Wesley's preaching when local Anglican congregations were not. And just as important, they provided a number of new Methodist societies with a significant nucleus of membership.

The Moravians

For the other form of *ecclesiola* that shaped early Methodism, Wesley was indebted to the Moravians, who influenced him considerably during his years in Georgia (1735-38) and for some time after his return. The history of the Moravian church goes back to the radical movements of late medieval Christianity, and in particular to the followers of the fifteenth-century Bohemian, John Hus. Originally named the *Unitas Fratrum* (the Unity of the Brethren), by the eighteenth century they had acquired an episcopal organization and a markedly ecumenical perspective.

They were continually persecuted, however, and frequently forced to move to new locations. The group on board ship with Wesley in 1735 came from a congregation that had been given a permanent home on the estates of Count Nikolaus Ludwig von Zinzendorf. In 1722 they had established a community named *Herrnhut* ("Watch of the Lord"), organized for the purpose of religious discipline. The members were divided into groups, or *classes*, according to age, sex, and marital status. In due course, these classes became known as *choirs*, subdivided into smaller groups, known as *bands*, to further their spiritual growth.

Wesley's encounter with them on the voyage to Georgia, which he sustained through periodic conversations during the next two years, was important for two reasons. First of all, it exposed him to their organization of small group fellowship and convinced him of its value. Not only did he adopt the format of the *bands* during his ministry in Savannah, but on his return to England in 1738 he incorporated them into the religious society which he and some Moravians formed at Fetter Lane in London, each band consisting of five to ten persons.

THE BANDS

As Methodist societies were formed elsewhere, bands were introduced as an integral part of their structure, and in December 1738 Wesley drew up a set of rules for their meetings.

These band rules were very searching indeed. They required the members to speak "freely and plainly" the true state of their souls, telling of the faults they had committed "in thought, word, or deed," and the temptations they had felt since their last meeting. Moreover, before persons were admitted to a band, they were asked a number of probing questions, such as:

- Have you peace with God, through our Lord Jesus Christ?
- Is the love of God shed abroad in your heart?
- Do you desire to be told of your faults?
- Do you desire that every one of us should tell you, from time to time, whatsoever is in his heart concerning you?
- Do you desire that, in doing this, we should come close as possible, that we should cut to the quick, and search your heart to the bottom?[16]

Clearly this was more than what today we would describe as "sharing." It was a process of mutual confession; and for those who took their discipleship seriously, as did the members of these early societies, it was a significant means of spiritual growth. At the same time, however, the bands had limitations, which began to emerge quite clearly once Methodist preaching took to the fields. Wesley noted that even with this weekly form of mutual confession, many of the new members were slipping back into their old way of life and even leaving the societies. By 1742 this was causing him considerable concern.

TOO MUCH TOO SOON

With the hindsight of modern research into small group dynamics, we can make an informed judgment as to why this happened: It was a case of cultural and spiritual disjunction. The bands, patterned after a Moravian community life which was refined and even sequestered, were too much too soon for ordinary working people. The pressing need of these new society members was not how to deepen their faith, but how to hang on to whatever faith they had, and how to live by it in the world.

For one thing, to talk about one's innermost spiritual life requires a vocabulary and an education that many ordinary people do not have even today, and certainly did not have then. To talk about deep feelings, and especially religious feelings, without the means to express them adequately must have led to considerable embarrassment, which in turn would have caused much apprehension about the next meeting. This alone would have been quite enough to cause people to stay away.

Another reason was that many of the people who joined the societies as a result of Methodist field preaching were unfamiliar with the church and its disciplines. They certainly had a deep faith, and their experiences of God's grace were ultimately to take their proper place in the spiritual treasury of the church. But Wesley discerned an important truth in these early years of the Methodist societies: The spiritual life must be kept in a proper relationship with the basics of Christian living in the world. Put differently, in authentic Christian discipleship, walking comes before running; and to walk steadily and consistently with Christ requires some basic habits and disciplines.

DISCIPLINED CHRISTIAN LIVING

While Wesley himself had spent years learning these disciplines, they presented an altogether new way of life for many of his new society members. Whether they had been dramatically converted or had merely begun to seek salvation, the reality of Christian living in a sinful world required them to have more than spiritual sensitivity. It required spiritual resilience. What was needed for the early Methodist movement, therefore, was a practical format for the building up of discipleship right where people were—*in* the world, not out of it.

Most of the people who joined the societies continued with their occupations—servants, farmers, craftsmen, shopkeepers—and therefore had to meet the challenge of Christian discipleship in the grist and grind of daily living. That Wesley recognized this and responded to it was not only a mark of his organizing genius, but also of his deep theological understanding of grace. And since grace is the key to his understanding of Christian discipleship, we need to look at it in some detail.

CHRISTIAN ASSURANCE
AND CHRISTIAN DISCIPLESHIP

Ironically, a good place to begin with this is the misunderstanding Wesley had with the Moravians at the Fetter Lane Society in 1740. The problem was sufficiently serious to cause a break in their relationship, and it ultimately led him to leave Fetter Lane and make his London headquarters at the Foundry.

One of the Moravian leaders, Philip Molther, had begun to insist that only a full assurance of faith was the mark of true salvation, and that until a person had experienced such an assurance, the only thing to do was to wait quietly for it to happen. Known as "Quietism," Wesley found this to be a mischievous teaching indeed. As a fine point of theological discussion, perhaps it had some merit. But as a guide for practical Christian living, it was little short of disastrous.

The issue was whether the assurance of faith was the same as salvation, or whether a sinner could receive forgiveness and reconciliation, irrespective of this particular religious experience. In a somewhat different form, it is the same issue that faces many of our congregations today: whether the significance of the gospel lies in what we do to respond to Christ or in what Christ has done for us; whether it is our faith in Christ which saves us or Christ himself.

DEGREES OF FAITH

Wesley opted firmly for the latter. He viewed salvation as by no means limited to a particular assurance of faith. There were *degrees of faith*, steps by which a person could be drawn to God. There were also *means of grace*, channels afforded by disciplines of the Christian life, through which a person could seek God. Moreover, these same means of grace were necessary to sustain Christian discipleship and bring it to maturity. People do not serve Christ by sitting aound waiting for grace to permeate their being. If they are waiting for God's blessings, they should do so actively, by feeding the hungry, clothing the naked, and visiting the prisons—just as Jesus taught (Matt. 25:31-40).

This tells us a great deal about Wesley's view of his ministry and about the structure of the early Methodist societies. In the refined seclusion of the Moravian settlement at Herrnhut, an emphasis on the assurance of faith was part of the structured life of the community. But in the realities of eighteenth-century England, a doctrine of salvation that depended primarily on religious experience was patently inadequate. The failure of the bands to provide a meaningful source of nurture for the membership as a whole had made this very clear. Bands were designed primarily for persons who were familiar with the life and teachings of the church, and for whom a deep religious experience came largely as an affirmation of all they had hitherto believed and practiced. But for those who became Methodists as newcomers to the faith, discipleship could not come merely from the assurance of faith. It had to come from *living it out*.

FORMS OF GRACE

To understand how Wesley applied this insight to the early Methodist societies, we must note first of all that he perceived God's grace to be active in the whole of human experience, and in every human being. It does, however, take a number of forms.

- *Prevenient Grace* invites the sinner to reconciliation with God, a process which gradually wears down the instinctive resistance of sinful human beings, until there is a despair, an "emptying" of self-sufficiency.

- *Justifying Grace* then establishes a new relationship with God, in which the human will finally submits to the divine initiative and the indwelling Spirit of God imparts a new life to the forgiven and reconciled sinner.

- This new life begins to develop immediately through the work of *Sanctifying Grace*, which changes the forgiven sinner from someone whose instinct is to resist God to someone whose instinct is to seek God. This does not happen all at once, but is a gradual transformation. It follows the "new birth" in Christ, just as physical growth follows the birth of a baby.

FREEDOM TO RESIST

A key element in Wesley's teaching on grace, however, is that God's grace will always give the freedom to resist grace. When prevenient grace is seeking to draw the sinner back to God, it is always possible to "quench" or to "stifle" these invitations of the Holy Spirit. Likewise, when justifying grace seeks the critical surrender of the sinner in a new relationship with God, the new birth can be impeded. And even when sanctifying grace is working the divine transformation of the sinner into a new person, it is possible to resist.

In other words, this new relationship with God is a continual choice. If the relationship is to be sustained, then it must be worked out in the world through an obedient discipleship. If the choice is disobedience, however, then the new relationship can be broken—and, if broken habitually, it can even be destroyed.

WESLEY'S "PELAGIANISM"

It was this teaching which caused many of the Calvinist evangelicals in the eighteenth-century Revival to brand Wesley as a Pelagian—someone who believes that salvation is by good works. For while these evangelicals viewed God's grace as irresistible (primarily, let it be said, for the commendable purpose of not giving any credit at all to sinful human beings for their own salvation) Wesley argued that grace was very resistible indeed. This in turn meant that human beings *do* have a part to play in their own salvation.

SALVATION WITH RESPONSIBILITY

In point of fact, Wesley's view was not really Pelagian, but what some theologians have labeled "synergistic"—the concept of cooperating with God's grace which Wesley found so vital in the early church.[17] His concern was not to deny the fullness of God's grace. His disagreement with the Calvinists was rather that their doctrine of irresistible grace denied proper responsibility to forgiven sinners. It is not that we can ever *earn* our new relationship with God. That is a gift, graciously bestowed by Jesus Christ. But we do have two things to do—one relatively easy, the other more difficult.

First, we must decide to accept our gift of salvation, our new relationship with God in Christ. That is a major threshold for us to cross, because it requires that we confess our sinful condition, have a change of heart, and come back home to God's family—what our forebears used to call conviction, repentance, and conversion. While this is a radical step for us to take, our part in it proves to be quite minimal. It is a matter of coming to our senses and accepting the obvious: We are God's estranged children, and we need to be reconciled. It is not so much our decision to come home, as God's pressing invitation that finally prevails. Our part is merely to decide not to refuse this invitation—at long last, to surrender to grace:

> His love is mighty to compel;
> His conqu'ring love consent to feel,
> Yield to his love's resistless power,
> And fight against your God no more.[18]

Our surrender to God's love is thus the easy part of our discipleship. The weight of our homecoming rests with God—the promptings, the pleadings, the entreaties, and supremely the invitation extended from the cross. The pain of our repentance and conversion is minor indeed compared to what God has done and is doing to bring the human family back home.

FAMILY CHORES

By contrast, the difficult part of our discipleship begins once we *are* back home—for coming home means that we are once again under the rules of the house. The welcome back has been generous, even lavish: parental greeting, reinstatement as heirs of the family, the fatted calf prepared for a feast, and everyone rejoicing to have us at the meal table again.

But then comes a rude awakening. Just when we want to lie in bed and continue to spend our time in self-indulgence (for there are clear benefits to being a prodigal—we would not have stayed away so long if there had not been); and just when we think we can slide back into our old habits, and do nothing but please ourselves, we are shaken out of our stupor with a sobering word: There are chores to be done!

Being back home not only means that we belong—it also means that we have to *behave* as if we belong. The privileges of once again being part of God's family carry the responsibility of pulling our weight along with everyone else. We cannot have the best of both worlds. Accepting this new relationship with Christ means that we must now fulfill some obligations in order to sustain it. That is the part of our salvation that requires a lifetime of work—and our work starts right away.

NECESSARY GOOD WORKS

In other words, when Wesley declared obedient discipleship to be necessary for salvation, it was not to earn salvation, but to *sustain* it. Good works are not the pre-condition of salvation, but the obligation and the privilege of those who have *received* salvation—if, that is, they wish to keep it.

It was this insistence on the necessity of good works which so many of Wesley's evangelical critics found objectionable. Instead of regarding Christian service as an outpouring of grace in the lives of faithful disciples, a consequence of their commitment to Christ, Wesley put the issue quite the other way around. Good works must be performed in order to maintain faithful discipleship—otherwise Christian disciples are by definition repudiating their new relationship with God, and breaking the covenant of their salvation.

A REVOLUTIONARY TEACHING

This was a revolutionary teaching in Wesley's day, even though its components were by no means new. On the one hand, Anglican theology had long pointed to the necessity of good works as a principle of the Christian life. On the other hand, Puritan theology had long argued for the central importance of a justified relationship with God, marked by the assurance of the inward witness of the Holy Spirit. But these had never before been put together in a practical, down-to-earth formula for Christian discipleship: A relationship with God is central to salvation, and good works are necessary to sustain it.

If we are honest with ourselves, this teaching is no less revolutionary today. Properly taught and applied, it could turn our congregations inside out.

CHRISTIAN MATURITY AND
CHRISTIAN OBEDIENCE

Given this insistence on good works in order to sustain our relationship with God in Christ, it can readily be seen how Wesley then proceeded to formulate the doctrine for which he is probably best known: the doctrine of Christian perfection, or Christian maturity. For the mark of a mature Christian, as Wesley defined it, is a consistent obedience to God, in which the new relationship of justifying faith is no longer interrupted by a wayward disposition, but firmly grounded in a service of love. It is a maturity in which the inward renewal of the believer has reached a point where obedient discipleship has become so habitual that the human will has lost its tendency to resist God's grace.

With this doctrine, Wesley brought his understanding of grace full circle. Preveniently there is a measure of grace in every human life, drawing each person to a new relationship with God. In our justification by Christ, there is a divine immediacy in every moment of our new relationship with God. This in turn is sustained by the sanctifying growth of faithful discipleship, which leads to a maturity of consistent obedience, marked by a perfect love that is as much a gift of God's grace as everything else in the life of the believer.

All of this is through grace upon grace upon grace. Our responsibility as disciples, therefore, must be to work at the continual task of deciding not to resist God's gracious initiatives in our lives.

ALDERSGATE STREET

This is why it is a mistake to view Wesley's Aldersgate Street experience as the most important turning point in his spiritual life. It was certainly a pivotal moment when, as he records in his *Journal,* his heart was "strangely warmed" at a small society meeting on the evening of May 24, 1738. But this was by no means his only deep religious experience, nor does he seem to have given it the prominence some biographers have subsequently ascribed to it. The assurance of faith he received that evening was indeed a direct witness of the Spirit of God. Yet it did not supersede his obligations as a Christian. Only by the disciplined practice of the Christian life could his new relationship with God in Christ be sustained.

SPIRITUAL DIVERSITY

Moreover, as he took the gospel the length and breadth of the land, Wesley saw the outpouring of God's grace in all of its dimensions. He found, in the richness of Methodist religious experience, a spiritual diversity that was analogous to birth, childhood, and coming of age. He saw people invited by God, "wooed" by God, and brought to the critical point of surrender. He saw their lives changed by justifying grace received through faith. When this was maintained in loving obedience, he saw the work of sanctifying grace, leading to the development of religious maturity—a perfection of love which Wesley came to regard as a "second blessing." When this maturity was taken for granted, however, there was a falling away, even by the most mature. Obedience could not for one moment be neglected.

✓ MUTUAL ACCOUNTABILITY

The critical question for Christian discipleship, therefore, was how to permit God's grace to foster a maturity of constant obedience, so that sanctifying grace might work with an unimpeded love. Wesley's theological understanding of this question led him to adopt what first seemed an unbelievably straightforward solution: a weekly meeting of like-minded persons who would exercise a mutual accountability for their discipleship.

He called this the *class meeting,* a "prudential means of grace" as profound as it was simple. Yet in adopting it as the basic format of the early Methodist societies, Wesley was not only being practical, he was drawing on years of theological searching. This weekly "form" of early Methodist discipleship, established in the earliest days of the movement, was based on the cardinal principle of grace: Authentic Christian discipleship consists of learning how not to say no to God. It remains the most important practical and theological contribution made by Wesley, and by Methodism, to the Christian tradition.

BASIC GUIDELINES FOR DISCIPLESHIP

By declaring that Christian discipleship is first and foremost a response to God's grace, Wesley was declaring that salvation does not lie in a striving for virtue, nor yet an experience of instant redemption. He could not regard those who did the best they could as beyond the scope of God's salvation any more than he could regard those with the second blessing as beyond the possibility of sin. Accordingly, his guidelines for the Methodist societies took the best of the Anglican religious societies and the Moravians, and then went further.

First, Wesley affirmed that while people respond to God's grace at various levels of resistance or acceptance, there are certain ways of serving Christ in the world that are so basic, they can be attempted by anyone who has the desire to do so, given the prevenient grace which all of us possess. These he called the "works of mercy" and defined them according to the guidelines of Jesus (Matt. 25:35-36) and those in the Epistle of James (2:14-17): To feed the hungry, clothe the naked, visit the prisons and the hospitals, and seek out those in need.

Wesley then went on to identify the basic spiritual disciplines through which all persons can further open themselves to God's grace, again regardless of the nature of their response. These he called the "works of piety," or "means of grace," ordained by the church and proven in practice. The minutes of the first Annual Conference in 1744 urged Methodist preachers to practice these disciplines, and to "enforce the use of them on all persons."

The *instituted* means of grace were listed as prayer (private, family, and public), searching the scriptures, the sacrament of the Lord's Supper, fasting, and Christian conference (what today we would call serious conversation about the will of God). The "prudential" means were those personal disciplines and forms of fellowship, such as the class meeting, which helped to ground the Christian in the basics of discipleship.[19]

THE FORM AND THE POWER OF DISCIPLESHIP

All of this came together in Wesley's leadership of the Methodist movement, a leadership which proved to have a highly distinctive quality. As he preached and taught and exhorted and admonished this growing "connection" of societies, Wesley emphasized not only the new relationship with God in Christ as the *power* of Christian discipleship, but also the works of mercy and piety as the *form* of Christian discipleship. Thus, whatever one's religious experience might be, and whatever degree of faith one might have received, *one could do one's best to be an obedient disciple, and know that it would be acceptable to God.*

Wesley stated this quite explicitly in his *General Rules* for the societies: The only precondition for admission to membership was a *desire* to be saved from sin, whether or not one could claim to have had a particular faith experience. To *continue* in a Methodist society, however, one had to give evidence of this desire: by avoiding evil, by doing good, and by using the means of grace, instituted by the church and proven in practice.

Since discipleship meant following the commandments of Christ according to the law of love, these rules could therefore be undertaken by anyone with right intent who was willing to follow some very basic guidelines. Not only those who loved the Lord Jesus Christ could become disciples; so could those who *wanted* to love him.

THE METHOD OF METHODIST DISCIPLESHIP

All of this leaves only one question outstanding, but it is the most critical question of all. Given the desire to be faithful Christian disciples, and given the commitment to accept the basic guidelines for faithful discipleship, how do we make sure that we actually follow them?

The answer to this is also to be found in the *General Rules*, which we shall examine in more detail in the next chapter. For the *Rules* stipulated not only the obligations of discipleship for the early Methodists, but also the method by which they were to carry them out—namely, that the members of each society were divided into "smaller Companies, called Classes, according to their respective

Places of abode," so that it might be "discerned whether they are indeed working out their own salvation."[20]

This terse statement of purpose does not beat about the bush. It tells us that the focus of early Methodism was first and foremost accountability in the Christian life. Yes, the society members enjoyed fellowship and community; and yes, they provided one another with significant spiritual nurture. But their priority was not to seek a religious experience. That came in due course as a gracious blessing. They were concerned first of all to pursue an obedience to Jesus Christ. Their commitment to mutual accountability expressed belief in a salvation that gave them freedom under God's grace, but also responsibility. They were charged to *work out* their own salvation.

THE CLASS MEETING

The weekly class meeting proved to be the most reliable way of doing this. It was a supportive structure for discipleship, grounded in the realities of daily living in the world, and undergirded by common sense. And, as we shall see, it proved to be the binding muscle of the early Methodist movement.

For Thought and Discussion

1. Which seemed more important to the early Methodists: faith or works?

2. What do you understand by the phrase "mutual accountability"?

3. What seem to have been John Wesley's strengths (a) as a theologian, (b) as a church leader?

4. What do you regard as the most important contribution to the development of early Methodism (a) by the religious societies, and (b) by the Moravians?

5. Can you find examples of *ecclesiola in ecclesia* in the church of today?

6. Would you find the mutual confession of the bands helpful for your discipleship? If not, why not?

7. Do you agree that Christian maturity (Christian perfection) is the development of a constant obedience to God?

8. Do you find "Necessary Good Works" (page 36) a revolutionary teaching?

Chapter 3

The Early Methodist Class Meeting

"THAT EXCELLENT INSTITUTION"

Once he perceived its usefulness and its validity, Wesley adopted the class meeting as the basic structure of all the Methodist societies. The idea emerged during a discussion in the Bristol society over a building debt. The date was February 15, 1742, and the account given by Wesley states that a retired seaman, known to us only as Captain Foy, proposed that each member of the society should give a penny a week toward clearing the debt. When it was pointed out that a penny a week was beyond the means of many members, he replied that he would personally accept responsibility for collecting the weekly amount from ten or twelve people in the society, and would make up any deficiencies himself. Others offered to do the same, and so it was agreed to divide the whole society into "little companies, or classes—about twelve in each class," with one person, styled as the leader, to collect the weekly contribution.[21]

"Thus began," as Wesley later described it, "that excellent institution . . . from which we reaped so many spiritual blessings that we soon fixed the same rule in all our societies."[22] The weekly class meeting proved to be the very thing that was needed to foster discipleship among the society members. As the leader visited the members to collect their money, something else began to happen. They began to give an account. They began to tell the story of what it had been like to be a faithful disciple during the past week.

LOTS TO TELL

There was a good reason for this. The early Methodists were often very lonely because they were marked people. To declare publicly that the commandments of Jesus Christ for personal and social behavior were to be taken seriously, and to pattern their lives accordingly, meant considerable tension with the world in which they lived. It meant "fighting the good fight of faith" in territory that was by no means neutral; and they certainly could not wage this fight alone.

When the weekly visit of the leader came around, therefore, they had lots to tell; and it was soon decided that, instead of the leader visiting each member, the members should meet as a group. In this way, not only was the leader saved the task of going around to collect the weekly contributions, but everyone could hear everyone else's account of their discipleship. In addition, the "advice, reproof, or encouragement" of the leader to individual members could benefit everyone. As a result, a dynamic of Christian fellowship quickly developed. They began to "watch over each other in love," and to hold one other accountable for their discipleship.

CRITERIA FOR ACCOUNTABILITY

Two criteria were established for this accountability: the *General Rules,* to which we referred in the previous chapter; and a time of questioning about the spiritual growth of the class members. Unfortunately, neither of these criteria has been well interpreted in the Methodist tradition. The *General Rules* have rarely been linked to the early Methodist classes, with the result that the fellowship and mutual support engendered by their weekly meetings have often been viewed as their primary purpose rather than a secondary benefit. By the same token, the criterion of spiritual questioning has often been interpreted as a time of open sharing, rather than the more particular spiritual evaluation which the early class leaders were asked to make on their attendance records.

Toward the end of Wesley's life, and certainly by the turn of the nineteenth century, the purpose of the class meeting did indeed become fellowship, sharing, and mutual support. But these were not its pristine objectives; and if we are to understand Wesley's intent for the original class meetings, we must examine each of his criteria for their accountability in some detail.

THE GENERAL RULES

Wesley first published the *General Rules* in 1743 as a set of guidelines for the societies as a whole. Printed as a small penny pamphlet, they went through thirty-nine editions in his lifetime, indicating that they were widely distributed among the members. Interestingly, the title page describes them as rules for the "United Societies." They did not carry the name "Methodist" until after Wesley's death in 1791. As we have noted, he was not particularly fond of the word.

The *Rules* are included in a number of modern Methodist *Disciplines*, but primarily as a historical document. This is unfortunate, because they are at once succinct and specific in their directives for Christian living in the world, and could easily be updated for modern use. A small pamphlet carried in the pocket would be a far more practical guide for daily living than the present *Book of Discipline*, with its 2,626 paragraphs!

DO NO HARM

After a short preamble, outlining the nature and purpose of the Methodist societies, the *Rules* first instruct the members to do no harm, and to avoid evil "in every kind—especially that which is most generally practised." When Christian disciples take this injunction seriously, as did the early Methodists, then guidelines for daily living will inevitably be practical and down-to-earth. Indeed, as we read through this very detailed list, it often seems to be fastidious and, to Christians of another age, even quaint or pointless. Yet at the time it was drawn up, the list was highly relevant to the task in hand, and it provides an interesting commentary on early discipleship, to say nothing of eighteenth-century English life.

More important, as Wesley made clear in so many of his writings, it affirms that genuine discipleship is rooted in *living out* the faith. Although some of these rules might make us smile, such as the censure of "uncharitable or unprofitable conversation, particularly speaking evil of Magistrates or Ministers," there is little that could not be readily applied to the late twentieth century, if only we had the will and the commitment.

DO GOOD

Second, the *Rules* enjoined on the early Methodists to do good, "by being in every kind merciful after their power, as they have opportunity doing good of every possible sort and as far as is possible to all men." There followed a similar listing of what Wesley would often describe throughout his ministry as "works of mercy." His use of the word *mercy* here is scriptural, taken from the King James Version of the Bible (Ps. 23:6; Rom. 12:1; Phil. 2:1, etc.), and alludes to the compassion of God rather than to a strictly legal connotation. In a word, works of mercy are expressions of God's grace.

To make sure that grace prevails, however, even on a bad day, Wesley goes on to caution against "that enthusiastic doctrine of devils, that 'we are not to do good unless *our heart be free to it.'*" Society members should "trample under foot" this demonic teaching, which falsely relieves Christians of any obligation for which they do not feel a spiritual prompting. Wesley knew only too well from his own years of rigorous spiritual learning that promptings from God could easily be ignored, or even misinterpreted, due to ill temper or lazy disposition. Works of mercy are obligatory for Christian disciples, therefore, even when we are not in the mood for them!

We should also note under this section of the *Rules* that, in doing good to their fellow human beings, Methodists were instructed to take care of people's physical needs first—giving food to the hungry, clothes to the naked, and visiting or helping those who were sick or in prison (Mt. 25:35-39). Only then were they to minister to their spiritual needs.

THE ORDINANCES OF THE CHURCH

Third, the *Rules* required the members of the societies to "attend upon all the Ordinances of God: Such are The public Worship of God; the Ministry of the Word, either read or expounded; The Supper of the Lord; Private Prayer; Searching the Scriptures; and Fasting, or Abstinence." Wesley regarded these "works of piety" as equally vital for faithful Christian living—those prescribed practices of the church without which any attempt to pursue an authentic Christian discipleship was doomed to failure.

This section of the *Rules* indicates not only that Wesley perceived worldly service in the name of Christ to be ineffectual without the power of the Holy Spirit, but also that the spiritual disciplines of Methodism were firmly linked to the larger *ecclesia*, the Church of England. He developed his guidelines for the societies on the assumption that they were *ecclesiolae* (little churches) in an *ecclesia* (big church) where the wider questions of doctrine and order were already well established. Even for those members of Nonconformist churches who joined the societies, such as Congregationalists and Presbyterians, there were similar expectations. They were to fulfill their churchly obligations no less than parishioners of the Church of England.

THE MEANS OF GRACE

We noted in the previous chapter that these "ordinances," or prescribed practices of the church, were also identified by Wesley as "means of grace." They were not, however, the only disciplines he viewed as "means" or "channels" of grace. In the Disciplinary Minutes of the Conference (*The Large Minutes*), there is a comprehensive listing of "instituted" means of grace (i.e., the ordinances of the church) and "prudential" means (i.e., those personal disciplines that further advance our spiritual growth).

In much more detail than in the *General Rules*, we find the instituted means of grace stipulated here as:

1. Prayer—private, family, public; consisting of deprecation, petition, intercession, and thanksgiving; also family prayer.
2. Searching the Scriptures—by reading, meditating and hearing; a New Testament is always to be at hand.
3. The Lord's Supper—at every opportunity, with earnest and deliberate self-devotion.
4. Fasting—every Friday.
5. Christian Conference—right conversation, 'seasoned with salt'; always with a determinate end in view, and with prayer before and after.[23]

The prudential means of grace are likewise listed in detail, those "particular rules" that help the Christian in the "arts of holy living." Examples of these are: class and band meetings; a "steady watch against the world, the devil, and besetting sins"; self-denial and temperance in all things; dietary habits ("Do you drink water? Why not? Did you ever? Why did you leave if off? If not for health, when will you begin again? Today?"); and cheerfully bearing our cross as a gift from God. The more we use these prudential means, the more we will grow in grace.[24]

GRACIOUS WORKS

Perhaps the most significant word throughout these guidelines is that Wesley described all of the disciplines as *works:* works of mercy and works of piety. The implication is profound. By *doing* these things, we open ourselves to grace. This is not to say that we can earn God's grace. That would be a contradiction in terms. But it is to say that we can so order our lives that we are more receptive to grace, more open to grace; that there are means, or channels, through which we can receive grace more abundantly.

Indeed, in this sense, the works of mercy are as much a channel of grace as the works of piety. Wesley argues forcefully for this elsewhere. Not only are our acts of compassion a means of grace, but neglect of them will weaken our faith, even though we continue in regular observance of the ordinances of the church. To sustain our faith, we must not merely talk with Jesus; we must walk with him.[25]

It was precisely this walk for which the early Methodists held themselves accountable at their weekly class meetings. Having set out on the narrow path of discipleship, they needed each other to keep their course straight and true. To have met for any other purpose would have been a waste of their time.

MATURITY OF OBEDIENCE

The second criterion for accountability in the class meeting was a questioning of class members about their spiritual growth. This was not the sort of intensive questioning that took place in the bands. There were too many variables in a class meeting for that. But spiritual growth was acknowledged to be both the sign and the result of obedient discipleship, and class leaders were asked to note on their records whether a member was still searching for faith ("awakened"), had experienced the new birth in Christ ("justified"), or had become mature in the faith ("perfected in love"). The nature of the class meeting might have been pragmatic and down-to-earth, but it certainly did not lack sensitivity to such mysteries of grace.[26]

FORMAT OF THE CLASS MEETING

This sensitivity was further evident in Wesley's concern to prevent the classes from becoming a mere formality. By their very nature, the weekly meeting had a fixed agenda; and while this provided a helpful structure for what took place, it also posed a danger.

The structure was helpful in that it kept the meetings focused on the task of Christian discipleship. Contemporary accounts clearly show that exchanges in the classes were largely catechetical, a process of question and answer between the leader and each member of the group. Meetings began with a prayer and a hymn; then the leader, starting with him or herself, asked all of the members in turn how they had kept the rules of the societies during the past week, and what was the state of their souls—how each one was faring in his or her spiritual journey. In response to the members' statements, the leader would articulate the points that could most profitably be shared by the others; and where appropriate, would offer comments of praise, reproof, or advice. It was a simple method, with precedents in the primitive church—and it was highly effective in fostering a Christian lifestyle among the members.

THE DANGER OF FORMALITY

The danger of such a structured format, however, was that the catechesis of question and answer might become monotonous, thereby stifling the dynamic of fellowship that developed as the class members became better acquainted with each other. Wesley was aware of this potential obstacle, and advised class leaders to vary the pattern of their questions, to encourage the spiritual progress of the members, and where possible to discern how God was at work in their lives. In this way, not only were the basic guidelines for discipleship fulfilled, but the group was able to share in the realities of each other's pilgrimage, and thereby in one another's growth toward spiritual maturity.

CONTINUATION OF THE BANDS

Needless to say, spiritual maturity was even more the agenda for band meetings, in which there was a much more informal exchange. It is important to note that the introduction of the class meeting did not bring an end to these earlier groups, which continued alongside the classes for those who needed the more intensive and searching process of mutual confession. They experienced a greater intimacy, due in large measure to Wesley's restriction of membership to those who wanted and needed "some means of closer union"; and it was here that the spiritual quest for Christian perfection was fostered and honed.

Accordingly, the bands were subjected to more rigorous disciplinary supervision than the classes. The preachers were instructed to meet with them weekly, and to be especially vigilant in enforcing the *Rules*. Band members received specially designated class tickets, marked with a letter "b," which were granted only after a trial period of three months. And band members were those in a society who were known to be well on the way to Christian maturity, the "path to perfection."

That the bands should have continued along with the classes also points to an important spiritual principle in Wesley's day and also in our own. While the early class meeting provided accountability for the basics of Christian discipleship, the more intimate and searching format of the band was still needed for inward spiritual growth.

BASIC STRUCTURE

Nevertheless, it was the class meeting which became the basic unit of Methodist organizational structure. While the bands were divided according to the Moravian pattern of age, sex, and marital status, the classes were formed by the much more down-to-earth and inclusive principle of topography. Men and women, young and old, married and single, all belonged to the class which met closest to where they and the leader lived. This served the very practical purpose of holding each member accountable for his or her discipleship—no more than this, but no less.

This pragmatic approach made the class meeting the most effective means of strengthening the discipleship of the membership as a whole. All Methodists, even if they were in a band, had to meet once a week with their class to give an account of their discipleship. It was an inclusive requirement, and it was an affirmation of grace. The "path to perfection" began *and continued* with an accountability for the basics of Christian discipleship, without which no genuine progress could be made in the Christian life.

THE CLASS LEADER

An important element in all of this was the class leader. Not only were class leaders crucial in a line of authority and communication extending from Wesley to the Methodist membership as a whole, but these men and women were also entrusted with a considerable responsibility for the spiritual welfare of the members. To preside at weekly meetings where people were asked to evaluate their discipleship was also to hold a great deal of power. Thus they were given very specific duties in the *General Rules*. And significantly, from an early date in the movement, women were appointed to this position as well as men.

While the appointment or removal of class leaders was the prerogative of Wesley and his assistants, this was not done arbitrarily. Leaders' authority depended to a large degree on the respect accorded by the class, not least because they were the ones who exacted accountability for everyone's discipleship. They met weekly with the preacher appointed by Wesley as minister of their society, both to report on their members, and themselves to receive advice and instruction. Their selection tended to evolve naturally as societies acknowledged their potential, and the progression from class leader to preacher was not uncommon. By the same token, Wesley and his assistants were quick to discern leadership qualities, and there is little question that they became as skilled a group of spiritual mentors as the church has ever produced.

CLASS DISCIPLINE

At a practical level, one of the most important tasks of the class leader was to report to the preacher if there were those who were disregarding the *General Rules;* and while critics have described these disciplinary measures as something of a police system, there was in fact a good reason for insisting on such strict supervision. In a small group fellowship, any lack of commitment or discipline on the part of an individual member was bound to be disruptive. If Methodists were to "watch over one another in love," then any member failing to provide this mutual support was certain to be a hindrance.

CLASS TICKETS

Wesley further enforced this discipline by introducing a relatively simple procedure, which at the same time provided society members with an important symbol of identity—*class tickets.* He adopted them initially at Bristol and Kingswood as a disciplinary measure to guard against "disorderly walkers," some forty of whom were expelled in February 1741. Similar disciplinary action was taken in London the following April, and thereafter he issued tickets to the membership of all the societies at a quarterly examination of the classes conducted by himself or one of his preachers. Those who were keeping the society rules were thereby provided with a visible means of encouragement, and at the same time those who were "walking disorderly" could be removed by withholding their new ticket.

This quarterly examination was a further means of supervising the leaders themselves. As we have noted, they were required to meet weekly with their preacher, to hand in class monies and to give a report on the progress of their members. But an examination of members by the preacher each quarter also provided an important check on how a leader was performing his or her task. Wesley makes this clear at many points in his correspondence, and in his journal and diary, where there are myriad references to his "visitations." His preachers were constantly directed to be thorough and conscientious in this aspect of their duties, and were under strict instructions to visit door-to-door those who were found not to have been meeting in class.

CONDITIONS OF MEMBERSHIP

The leaders were also the initial point of contact for those who wished to join a society. On the leader's recommendation, a note would be issued for admittance to society meetings; and at the end of the three months, the leader would again be consulted about full membership. Furthermore, just as the class meeting was the occasion of membership, it was also the condition. Regular attendance at the weekly meetings was one of the first items in the quarterly examination for the renewal of class tickets, and the preachers were given clear instructions to withhold tickets from those who were irregular. The general, though unwritten, rule was that three consecutive absences constituted self-expulsion from a class, and leaders were required to keep an accurate record of attendance. By the same token, when a new society was established, the formation of the first class was the immediate priority.

THE "MUSCLE" OF THE BODY

There is no better expression of the importance Wesley attached to class meetings than his description of them as the *sinews* of the Methodist societies.[27] While his use of this word was in the sense of "mainstay" or "chief supporting force," it also provides a vivid metaphor when we relate it to the Pauline image of the Body of Christ (Rom. 12; 1 Cor. 12). For if the body of the church has many limbs and organs, and each has its particular function as in a physical body, then the idea of "sinews" gives a very particular role to the class meeting. Strictly speaking, sinews are those strong, fibrous chords that bind the muscle of the body to the bone, or serve as tendons. But if we adapt the metaphor a little, and refer to class meetings as the "muscle" of the body, we have a powerful image indeed.

For one thing, muscle is present throughout the body. We have muscles not only in our limbs, but also in places such as our neck, our lips, and even our ears. In fact, muscle is what gives the body the ability to move and the strength to act. For another thing, muscle works silently, and is largely hidden. There is evidence of it, of course (indeed, at body-building contests, much evidence of it!), but it remains concealed under the skin. Muscle is altogether integral to the body as a whole.

One thing more: when muscle is not used, it becomes flabby, and eventually turns into excess fat, demanding life from the rest of the body, but giving nothing in return.

✔ BODY BUILDING

There are many more ramifications to this imagery beyond the scope of our present study. Suffice it to note, therefore, that the class meeting is one of the best examples we have of Wesley's theological acumen and practical churchmanship at work together: Wesley the theologian, concerned for the building up of the Body of Christ; and Wesley the evangelist in the field, concerned for the building up in the faith of those who responded to the gospel.

In both respects, we find a deep understanding of the New Testament word *oikodomé*—the edification or building up of faith, both in the individual believer and in the body of the church (Rom. 15:2; 1 Cor. 14:26; Eph. 4:29). If we extend all of this imagery even further, we might say that the class meeting was a means of "body building"—developing the strength of the body by using its muscular potential. At this point, the image of a church whose muscle has not been used for some time becomes painfully clear to those of us in present-day North America.

THE BODY OF THE CHURCH

In the final analysis, Wesley's use of the word *sinew* perhaps has a greater significance than he himself intended. It is not only a good descriptive word. It is also a physical word, tying the class meeting to the body of the church as a whole, and making the point that authentic discipleship could not be practiced without seriously taking into account the reality of the visible church. This church, instituted by Christ, and going all the way back in Christian tradition to the apostles themselves, was not of course without its faults. It was divided; it had often been unfaithful; and in Wesley's day, its particular expression in the Church of England was, to say the least, lethargic. Yet in spite of its imperfections, and however much it may have erred in its service to Jesus Christ, it had prevailed across the ages, and still prevails.

For anyone answering the call to Christian discipleship, therefore, in our own day no less than in Wesley's, the church remains not only as a conceptual framework for the task in hand, but is also inescapably present. It is corporal, historical fact.

THE DECLINE OF THE CLASS MEETING

Given the importance of the class meeting in early Methodism, we are bound to ask why it is no longer the foundation of Methodist polity and practice. Although there were some specific historical factors contributing to its decline (dealt with in the companion volume, *Class Leaders*, order #DR092), the main reason for the disappearance of the class meeting is quite simple: Methodism became a church. This may sound trite; but in fact it is an aspect of Methodist history which is critical to our self-understanding, not only with regard to our forebears in the faith, but also with respect to our present Christian obligations.

FROM SOCIETY TO CHURCH

In essence, the transition from small, highly selective societies, to a large, inclusive church, meant that accountability for Christian discipleship could not be exercised in the same way. It was not that joining one of Wesley's societies was an exclusive process—the doors were open wide for any persons who wanted to be saved from their sins. The selectivity came with the condition of *remaining* in a society; and it was always a process of self-selection. If people were willing to keep the rules, then they were welcome—if not, then they had to leave. It was that simple, and that inflexible.

The contrast between those early societies and the Methodist congregations we now have can best be illustrated by asking some simple but searching questions: How many pastors of today would be willing to subject their members to a quarterly examination for continuing membership? How many would insist on regular attendance at midweek meetings? How many would want to check on the behavior of members through the oversight of someone like a class leader? For that matter, how many members would submit to such conditions? We know what the answers would be; for whenever these questions are asked in a contemporary workshop setting, there is invariably a burst of incredulous laughter.

KEEPING THINGS IN CONTEXT

If we are to draw any lessons from Wesley's class meeting for the church of today, therefore, we must do so through a process of contextualization. First, we must keep the early Methodist societies in their eighteenth century context, remembering that they were never a mass movement in Wesley's day. In 1766, the first year for which we have collected statistics, they numbered only some 19,000 in England and Wales, a growth rate of fewer than 14 per week across the nation. Even at Wesley's death in 1791, when the societies had begun to make large strides in urban areas, there were still only some 53,000 out of a population estimated to be between 8.5 and 9 million.[28]

We must also keep the contemporary United Methodist Church in its late twentieth century context, remembering that it is a major Protestant denomination with a membership very close, as it happens, to the population of England and Wales at the close of Wesley's life. We cannot equate this modern United Methodist Church with Wesley's Church of England; but in a very real sense, the challenge we face today can be compared with that which faced the early Methodists.

TO REFORM THE CHURCH

As Wesley saw the task, Methodism was meant to be a reforming movement within the large, inclusive church. The tragedy of his ministry (and tragedy is not too strong a word) is that an obstinate Church of England, a vital evangelical revival, and the course of political events in North America, all contributed to the formation of a new denomination—something which, as we noted in the previous chapter, he resisted in England as long as he lived.

But today, in the late twentieth century, and with all the benefits of accumulated hindsight, we can and should know better. United Methodists are not the same as the Church of England in Wesley's day, but we have the same symptoms of a large, inclusive church, which badly needs role models and leaders in discipleship. The function of the large *ecclesia* is always to be a ready means of grace for everyone, whatever their response to the gospel of Jesus Christ. But the function of the small *ecclesiola* is to set the pace of that response for the body of the church as a whole.

ECCLESIOLA *AND* ECCLESIA

This is what makes our early Methodist forebears such important role models for discipleship today. They did not expect everyone in the Church of England to become Methodist. They knew that their calling, their experience, and their way of life were very particular and had little popular appeal. Moreover, no one knew better than Wesley himself that the great majority of Anglican clergy would remain disdainful of what was happening in the societies, classes, and bands.

Our debt to these early Methodists—and it is a considerable debt—is that they strove to integrate their witness with the mission of the larger church. This is not to say that their striving was consistent. There were a number of occasions when the impulse to form a separate denomination was strong indeed, and was barely averted.[29] But under Wesley's leadership, they never lost sight of the larger purpose of their calling, which was "to reform the nation, particularly the Church; and to spread scriptural holiness over the land."[30]

COMMITMENT TO THE CHURCH

This dimension of the early Methodist movement tends to be overlooked when we fail to take seriously what it meant for our forebears to be faithful disciples in their day, and apply their learnings to our own task of discipleship. We place so much value today on personal choice that many of our congregations have become little more than voluntary associations, in which people stay only as long as their needs are being met, and from which they feel very free to part company when they become dissatisfied. By contrast, Wesley viewed the church as ordained of God and worthy of our loyalty and commitment, whatever its condition might be. Schism (i.e., causeless separation from a body of living Christians) he regarded as "both evil in itself, and productive of evil conse-quences."[31]

As we know, Methodism ultimately became a separate church, first of all in North America—with good reason and with Wesley's blessing. That is not the issue today, however. What we rather have now are voluntaristic, personalized separations of attitude and outlook. Structural separation would be counterproductive; on that we are agreed. But mentally, emotionally, and even spiritually, we have many examples of persons who, wishing to take their disci-pleship more seriously than their fellow church members, opt for a Christian mindset that pays lip service to their congregation, but which deep down disdains its teachings, its leadership, and its lifestyle.

THE CHALLENGE OF EARLY METHODISM

It is in this sense that we face the same challenge that confronted the early Methodists: How to be a faithful Christian disciple, yet stay with integrity in the larger church? If we wish to learn from our forebears, we must remember their *Rules* as well as their spiritual fervor. We must observe the balance they held between works of mercy and works of piety. We must emulate their mutual accountability as well as their rich communion. But more than anything else, we must continue their joint commitment to the *ecclesia* and the *ecclesiola* of their societies.

For in that commitment lies their challenge for the task of our discipleship today. Will those of us who are ready to become ac-countable disciples of Jesus Christ dedicate our commitment to the ministry and mission of the church in the world? Or will we use it primarily for personal ends—even when those ends are dedicated to the service of Jesus Christ?

For Thought and Discussion

1. The weekly class meeting was a point of accountability for the early Methodists. Why do you think it is no longer a requirement for church membership?

2. Do you agree that "works of mercy" and "works of piety" are equally important in the Christian life?

3. Would class tickets be practicable for local congregations today? If not, why not?

4. Which seems to have been more important for the early Methodist societies: the band or the class meeting?

5. Do you think that the office of the early Methodist class leader could prove useful in the church today?

6. Do you find "sinews" and "muscle" (pages 53-55) helpful images? In what ways?

7. Do you think that Methodists have accepted the identity of church rather than society?

8. How would you address the challenge of giving costly discipleship a proper role in the church of today?

Chapter 4

The Class Meeting
For the Church of Today

TRADITIONING THE CLASS MEETING

We began this study with the observation that many Christians today are ready to make a disciplined commitment to their discipleship. They reject the option of a lukewarm folk religion, which demands little of the believer and offers all sorts of personal benefits the church was never meant to provide—with an appalling wear and tear on its human and material resources. At the same time, they are uncomfortable with a radical Christian manifesto which seems to present impossible demands, and which raises serious questions about the extent to which it is a work of grace.

We also observed that these tensions are by no means new. Christian disciples have been confronted by the challenge of their witness in every age, and there have never been easy answers. It has always been difficult to sustain a faithful Christian witness in the world, because the world is not yet the kingdom of God. Sin is still rampant, and a sinful world will always resist the coming new age of Jesus Christ. In this regard, the late twentieth century is no different from any other time.

The purpose of looking at our Methodist heritage, therefore, has not been to seek easy solutions by copying blueprints that were drawn up for an earlier age. Rather, we have asked how our forebears met this same challenge of discipleship in their time, to see whether they have something to teach us. Certainly some of the problems they faced are strikingly similar to our own. There was tremendous social upheaval as the early industrial revolution began to uproot people from the countryside and overcrowd the cities. This was accompanied by economic uncertainty, a great deal of poverty, and a resultant wave of crime. The response to this was a penal code, the conditions of which we would regard today as savage, but the demands for which are all too familiar.

Social factors, however, are not the only or even the major occasion of our sense of identification with the early Methodists. What links us is our oneness of the call to discipleship in the power of the Holy Spirit. As we have noted, it is ultimately impossible to correlate the eighteenth century with the twentieth. But if we ask some pertinent questions about their discipleship, in particular with regard to the mutual accountability of their class meetings, we will find a great deal that is important for our present task.

ACCOUNTABILITY
FOR CHRISTIAN DISCIPLESHIP

The key to understanding the dynamic of the early class meeting is the word *accountability*. As we have noted, the members developed an openness to one another, and an intimacy that permitted them to share their spiritual pilgrimage unreservedly. Yet it is a mistake to assume that the class meeting was what today we would call an intensive group experience. This was much more the character of the bands.

The first priority of the class was rather to "watch over one another in love." But if we emphasize the love which they shared to the exclusion of the mutual accountability which they exercised, both for the means of grace and for the obedience of their discipleship, we misunderstand the purpose and function of these weekly meetings. The *General Rules* put it well. Methodists were those who, "having the Form, and seeking the Power of Godliness, united in order to pray together, to receive the Word of Exhortation, and to watch over one another in Love, that they may help each other to work out their Salvation."[32]

ACCOUNTABILITY FOR LIVING IN THE WORLD

There were many small group movements in Wesley's day, and many aspects of the Evangelical Revival were seemingly more successful than his. But Methodism prevailed because the bedrock of the early societies was an active witness *in the world*. These Methodists did not seek pleasant surroundings on weekends in order to "find God." They knew that God had found them right where they were. The earliest Methodist classes had nowhere else to meet but where the members lived and worked. And they gathered week by week because they knew that when the prayer was given and the hymn was sung, God was present in the power of the Holy Spirit, and was there to bless.

Moreover, they knew that when they resumed their "daily round and common task," God would be there ahead of them. Far from running away from the world, the class meeting helped the early Methodists to view their surroundings in a new light. By grace, they had the eyes to see—and they needed grace, how they needed it! For to be a Methodist was all too often to be subject to ridicule, disdain, persecution, and frequently personal assault. To live out a Methodist witness in the crowded urban areas which were so rapidly spreading in eighteenth century England, or in the villages with their tight community life, was to be under scrutiny at every turn. The words of the hymn, which Charles Wesley wrote for them to sing on their way to work, take on new meaning when we remember what they faced:

> Forth in thy name, O Lord, I go,
> My daily labor to pursue;
> Thee, only thee, resolved to know
> In all I think or speak or do.[33]

ACCOUNTABILITY FOR THE GENERAL RULES

It is worth noting that there is no mention of Wesley's Aldersgate Street experience in the *General Rules*. Nor, in fact, is there any reference to being "born again." This is not to say that Wesley regarded the new birth as unimportant. Quite the contrary, he gave it prominence in the *Large Minutes,* which served as a sort of book of discipline for the societies; and he gave it priority in many of his sermons, some of which were devoted entirely to the importance of the new birth in the spiritual life.[34]

Wesley was also at pains to stress, however, that this experience must quickly be outgrown. The milk of spiritual infancy must be replaced by the meat of discipleship, of disciplined Christian living in the world. He was not in favor of keeping Methodists on a permanent diet of Gerber Foods! Thus the *General Rules* took for granted that the new birth would be experienced by society members, in God's good time and by God's good grace. However, there were things to be done for Jesus Christ, both before and after conversion, which on the one hand could help to prepare for this assurance of the indwelling Spirit of God, and on the other hand could enable a person to grow in the grace of that assurance.

ACCOUNTABILITY FOR WORKS OF MERCY

Accordingly, the *General Rules* stipulated a balance between works of mercy and works of piety; and the weekly class meeting was a means of ensuring that the balance was in fact being kept in the daily lives of the members. The most interesting instruction concerning all of this is the significant sentence we have already noted, that Methodists were to "trample under foot that enthusiastic doctrine of devils, that we are not to do good unless our heart be free to it."

The teaching which Wesley described as devilish is still around today. Essentially it states that, since it is God's Spirit who empowers all of our good works, we should only do those things which the Holy Spirit prompts us to do—that is, about which our hearts are free. If we were all saints, living in a perfect world, this might be feasible. But since most of us remain a questionable mixture of sin and sanctity, it is a very dangerous teaching indeed. At best, it instructs us to wait for a high spiritual moment before we do anything to help our neighbor. At worst, it is saying that we need only do good works when we are in the right mood.

Wesley wanted his members to be very clear on this point. There are good works to be done, whether or not we are in the right mood. How do we know this? Because Jesus left us with some very clear guidelines: to feed the hungry, clothe the naked, help the sick, and visit the prisons. So let's get on with it. And as we do, we will probably bump into Jesus, who is of course there ahead of us.

ACCOUNTABILITY FOR WORKS OF PIETY

We have already noted that works of piety, or means of grace, are those habits and disciplines which, while they do not manufacture grace, help us to keep our channels to God open. To put it another way, by following these well-tried spiritual practices and exercises of the church, we can play a part in breaking down our resistance to grace, and thus be more in tune with God's will. Wesley wanted the class members to be clear about the need to be constantly open to God's grace; so he stressed the means of grace in the *Rules*, and required the class members to be accountable each week for using them.

WORKING FOR OUR SPIRITUAL FOOD

It seems incongruous to describe these disciplines as "works" of piety, since the essential meaning of grace is an unmerited gift from God. Yet there is an important parallel here with our physical existence. When we are infants, we receive our nourishment from our parents; but when we become adults, we have to work for our food. The same is true in the Christian life. We cannot expect God to breastfeed us all the time. We must learn to acquire those habits and follow those disciplines that earn us our food. In one real sense, of course, any food is a gift from God. That is why we give thanks at the mealtable before we begin to eat. But by the same token, someone has had to work to put the food on the table—and thus the "works" of piety in the *General Rules*.

We should note something else about these works of piety. Some were to be done individually, in private; but others were to be done publicly in company with other Christians. There is an important principle here: the impossibility of trying to be a Christian disciple on one's own. Wesley regarded solitary Christianity as a contradiction in terms, and he constantly warned the class members of the grave risk in trying to live out their faith without the help of others. Regular attendance at the class meeting was thus an absolute requirement, a "prudential means of grace," which they neglected at their peril.

ACCOUNTABILITY TO AND FOR THE CHURCH

Because Wesley insisted that the Methodist societies remain within the Church of England, the class meeting became a twofold point of churchly accountability. First of all, it held the members of the classes accountable *to* church discipline. They were committed to availing themselves of the instituted means of grace, those disciplines of the church through which grace might be received. Methodists were not only instructed to practice them. They were also known for doing so.

But at the same time, the class meeting was a point of accountability *for* the church. The Methodists were actually doing what the teachings of the church encouraged faithful Christians to do, but which most parishioners and many clergy had failed to heed for years, if ever they had. They were thus representing the church in the world far more effectively than many of their Anglican critics. Indeed, in a very real way they were accepting responsibility for a delinquent church.

It was this which Wesley regarded as one of the most important reforming influences of the Methodist movement—calling the church back to the principles of scriptural Christianity, to personal holiness and to social responsibility, through its own ordinances.

ACCOUNTABILITY TO THE HOLY SPIRIT

Accountability to and for the church left the Methodist societies and classes free in turn to respond to the promptings of the Spirit as they took their message and their witness the length and breadth of the land. By affirming the structure of the large church, the *ecclesia*, Methodism functioned as a collection of little churches, *ecclesiolae*. Thus they were unencumbered by churchly responsibilities, and were able to pursue an active discipleship and spiritual witness in the world.

Without Wesley's constant endeavor to sustain this structural relationship to the Church of England, the societies might indeed have been vulnerable to the charges of "enthusiasm" (i.e., religious fanaticism) which were leveled at them. For the directness of the inward spiritual witness which Wesley understood so well as the dynamic of true discipleship, and which he was at such pains to foster through he classes and the bands, could also be a pitfall. It could, and often did, lead to spiritual self-sufficiency, or even spiritual arrogance. There were plenty of examples of this in Wesley's day; and even though his critics did not bother to make the distinction between Methodists and "enthusiasts," he constantly took steps to guard against this religious fanaticism in his societies.

Indeed, the genius of Wesley's leadership of the Methodist movement lay not only in his organizational skills, but also in the way he held the society members accountable for their spiritual gifts without in any way questioning the authenticity of their spiritual experiences. He affirmed time and again that the inward witness they received was that of the Holy Spirit, and not just religious fervor. For an Anglican cleric of his day, this was an exceptional insight—though immediately recognizable to anyone who, like himself at Aldersgate Street, had received that very gift.

At the same time, he understood the importance of grounding this experience in the teachings of the church; for the spirit of authentic inward witness is always the Holy Spirit, the Spirit who is one with God and with Christ. It mattered less, therefore, what sort of religious experience these society members had received, or whether they had yet received an experience at all. What counted was a willingness to join with others of like purpose in living out an obedient discipleship in the world. Growth in grace, the new birth, and the gift of the "second blessing"—all of these ensued, and were actively anticipated. But to sustain a living faith, they knew that first they had to develop an obedience to the Spirit of God, many of whose guidelines for daily living were to be found in the teachings of Jesus. Dedicated application to these tasks was the mark of a faithful disciple no less than spiritual gifts.

THE METHOD OF METHODISM

In all of these ways, the class meeting helped the early Methodists to exercise accountability for their discipleship—the method of their Methodism. Some of their customs and practices were clearly peculiar to the context of eighteenth-century England. But many more are strikingly familiar to those of us who endeavor to face the challenge of discipleship in the late twentieth century.

We must follow the example of the early Methodists, therefore, in one further dimension. We must ask not only whether the early class meeting can help us in our discipleship today, but *how* it can.

ACCOUNTABLE DISCIPLESHIP FOR TODAY

Before we do so, it is important to remind ourselves one more time that we cannot go back to Wesley's model and copy it. Eighteenth-century England cannot be transferred to twentieth-century North America; nor, for that matter, can it be transferred to twentieth-century England. But it is possible to *tradition* the class meeting—that is, we can try to understand it in its own context in light of the gospel, and then appropriate it for contemporary Christian discipleship. In this way, perhaps a new plant can grow in the soil of a different time and place.

TWO IMPORTANT CONTEXTUAL FACTORS

We also need to remind ourselves of two important contextual factors as we proceed with this traditioning. The first is that the movement which began with the Wesley brothers is now 200 years old as a church. As we shall see, this has some profound implications for how we view the class meeting as a paradigm for our discipleship.

The second factor is that we happen to live in a culture today where small groups have become recognized as useful and necessary components of our social fabric. This includes the church, where they serve to strengthen and sustain the spontaneity of fellowship—best described by the scriptural word *koinonia*—and where they also provide an important format for adult education.

While there is no doubt that these groups accomplish much for our church members, especially for those who look to the church for the community they cannot find elsewhere in an impersonal, technological society, we must remember that there was much more to the early Methodist class meetings than fellowship. These weekly gatherings were first and foremost designed to equip Christians to be authentically Christian in a world that was largely hostile to their message. The early Methodists believed they had received a direct commission to go into the world and to join the risen Christ in the task of proclaiming God's salvation in the power of the Holy Spirit. The class meeting was where they came to share the bumps and bruises of this encounter, to comfort and strengthen one another, and to provide a mutual accountability for the task in hand.

If we keep these factors in mind as we apply the class meeting to our discipleship today, they will help us not to draw inappropriate conclusions—the most frequent mistake in traditioning the gospel. They will also point us to some unexpected possibilities.

MUTUAL ACCOUNTABILITY

Of all the "commonsense" virtues of the class meeting, mutual accountability is the most important. We know what it is like to be around people whose schedule runs like clockwork, whose homes are immaculate, who seem to find their work effortless, who are involved with community projects, who never lack the time for issues of social justice, and who are always, infuriatingly, correct. There is an aura of unreality about them. They seem to be super-human, and in an altogether different league.

By contrast, most of us find it difficult to get organized for anything other than day-to-day survival. This is why the idea of mutual accountability—of joining with other people of like mind and purpose in order to make our discipleship more effective—is so logical. It is not so much a recipe for success as it is just plain, practical common sense.

If we take a moment to consider, we can see that this approach is widely used today in a number of settings. We noted some examples in Chapter One, and others come immediately to mind. People who wish to exercise will find a partner for jogging, tennis, or aerobics. People who wish to sharpen their understanding of a subject will discuss it together and perhaps form a book club or a lunch group. Repairing a car or a roof, or clearing out a garage, seems to be put off indefinitely until we ask a friend to help us. And who wants to go to a ballgame or a concert alone?

ONE DAY AT A TIME

The clearest examples of mutual accountability today, however, are Alcoholics Anonymous, Weight Watchers, and the myriad other groups these organizations have spawned. They are made up of people who face a common problem, who have acknowledged it, and who have agreed to help one another cope with it. Members of these groups will never say they have overcome the problem, for alcoholics and compulsive eaters will remain that way for the rest of their lives. They can reach a point, however, where they sustain a resistance to their problem; then, by living one day at a time, they can achieve a moment-by-moment victory.

So it is with those who call ourselves Christian disciples. Our problem is that we are sinners, all of us; and sinners we shall remain until our salvation in Christ has been brought to fulfillment in the new age of God's reign on earth as in heaven. We know we are forgiven and reconciled sinners, accepted by God *just as we are.* But we also know that our forgiveness holds a promise—the call to grow in our discipleship.

Those who receive this forgiveness and hear this promise have come to a deeper knowledge of our problem, and have acknowledged the need to sustain our new life in Christ. We know we will grow in grace only to the extent that we are obedient in our discipleship. The choice is always ours: whether to accept or to resist God's gracious initiatives in our lives. Likewise the choice is ours of which method to use in learning how to follow Christ consistently.

HOLDING FAST WITH ONE ANOTHER

The early Methodists discovered that mutual accountability—holding fast in company with one another—was a very good method for building up a consistent discipleship. It is as relevant today as it was 200 years ago. We have looked at it thus far in the format of their class meetings. But we can also see it in a sampling of headings from their 1780 hymnal: "Praying for Repentance," "For Mourners convinced of Sin," "For Mourners brought to the Birth," "For Believers Rejoicing, Fighting, Praying, Watching," "Convinced of Backsliding," and "Recovered."[35]

Those of us accustomed to the comforts of modern counseling might find such concepts rather off-putting. Who, we might wonder, would ever admit in a modern congregation to being a "backslider" or to "recovering" from such a state? Indeed, who would ever think of asking such a question of a fellow church member? Until, that is, we think of Alcoholics Anonymous and Weight Watchers. If one of their members happens to "fall off the wagon," or "pig out," does the group not rally round? And when the "backslider" has "recovered" from the stumble, is there not "more rejoicing over the one than over the ninety-and-nine"?

Our problem today is that we think we have outgrown the snares of sinful human nature in a sinful world. But nothing could be farther from the truth. Notwithstanding all our modern expertise in human personhood, we have no idea what it means to follow Christ so consistently that to stumble would be a catastrophe. Our problem is very basic, and our Methodist forebears would have diagnosed it for us in an instant: We have nothing to backslide from!

MEETING WITH JESUS CHRIST IN THE WORLD

The class meeting can further guide our discipleship by reminding us of the center of our faith: God became a human being. We frequently overlook the significance of this, though the early Methodists did not. They lived it; they sang about it; and they proclaimed it throughout the land.

Because God had become a human being, they knew that the world was acceptable to God and worth saving from its evil. They knew that the human race was acceptable to God and worth saving from its sin. And because God came as a servant to the human race, they knew that faithful Christians were called to follow Christ's example in service to the world. They saw better than most that to live faithfully in the world was quite simply to meet Christ where he was to be found: in their towns and villages, in their places of work, and in their homes, where most of the early class meetings were held. They knew that discipleship was not nearly so much a quest *for* God as a willingness to be found *by* God, right where they were; and then a readiness to be obedient.

SERVING JESUS CHRIST IN THE WORLD

This paradigm of worldly discipleship is not only the living of a good life. That is the duty of any self-respecting member of the human race, and applies to Christians no less than to anyone else.

For the disciple, however, the task goes further. In addition to living a good life, there is the obligation to be obedient to Jesus Christ. This is a task at once more demanding and difficult to discern, because it may well present us with a choice between doing the will of Christ or pursuing those ideals which come close to Christian discipleship, but which ultimately miss it by a mile. The distinctive duties of our discipleship will go beyond our service to others, and even beyond our devotional life. They will lie rather in serving those whom Jesus specifically wishes us to serve, at those times and in those places specifically determined by Jesus—all of which makes our discipleship very particular, and therefore requires it to be highly disciplined.

Learning this discipline takes a lifetime. But the most important lesson must be learned at an early stage: Christian discipleship does not take us out of the world. It is most certainly life-changing, and it marks us as persons with highly distinctive loyalties. But we remain human, like everyone else. There are many hours of the day when we live like every other human being, breathing, eating, walking, talking—doing all those familiar activities common to the human race. Moreover, even when we behave according to the teachings of Jesus—helping those in need, or speaking out for the disadvantaged—we often find ourselves working alongside human colleagues who are not Christian, but are doing just as good a job as we are. Indeed, they often do a much better job, as Jesus pointedly illustrated with the parable of the good Samaritan (Luke 10:25-37).

ON CALL FOR CHRIST

The discerning Christian therefore quickly comes to realize that discipleship is not so much a constant task as it is to be on constant call. At any time, Jesus may require a particular act of compassion, a particular word of justice, or a particular refusal to act or speak. The disciple must be ready for these instructions, which usually come as promptings of the Holy Spirit. As we shall suggest in the next chapter, developing a sensitivity to these promptings and fostering obedience to them is one of the most important dimensions of our discipleship. For they direct us to what Jesus needs doing or saying at particular times and places—the high privilege of our calling.

ACTIVE EXPECTANCY

This does not mean, however, that we wait around idly for grace to strike. Being on constant call for Christ also means getting on with the job of courteous and considerate living in the world, according to the teachings of Jesus laid out very clearly in the New Testament. In this way, we will be properly prepared for the special assignments of Christian discipleship.

Christians should be suspicious, therefore, of any activity which suggests that a retreat from the world is the way to God. Yes, we all need to develop our spiritual life; and yes, there are times when this can only be done in a context of relaxation and recreation. But God is no more present at those times than in the daily grist and grind of our work and in the familiar nooks and crannies of our homes; indeed, sometimes much less so.

"I Found It!" we used to read on car bumper stickers. On the contrary, it is God who finds us, *wherever* we are. It is God who calls us, from time to time, as faithful disciples to particular and critical service. And it is God who commends us when we are found ready for the task (Luke 12:35-48).

THE NEED FOR BASIC GUIDELINES

This twofold approach to Christian discipleship—living in the world according to the teachings of Jesus, but also being ready for the particular call to service—is clearly reflected in the *General Rules*. Throughout our study, these rules have emerged as the framework and the guidelines of early Methodist discipleship. They are basic and straightforward, and might even be regarded as legalistic by Christians who are less mature and seasoned than the early Methodists. Indeed, there were many evangelicals in the eighteenth century who said as much. Methodists needed rules, they charged, because they were short on grace!

When Wesley wrote these *Rules* for the Methodist societies, however, legalism was by no means his purpose. The man whose heart had been strangely warmed at Aldersgate Street could never be accused of that. In their daily living, Methodists were as aware as any, and more aware than most, of the dynamic presence of the Holy Spirit. The point of the *General Rules* was to make clear that the privilege of spiritual promptings did not excuse the obligations of Christian living in the world. They had the common sense to understand that without the safeguard of some basic guidelines for the "daily round and common task," spiritual pursuits can render a person "too heavenly minded to be of any earthly use." And the taunts they received from their evangelical cousins further confirmed that the first symptom of spiritual pride is almost always rank bad manners in the ordinary things of life.

To apply the lessons of early Methodism to our present task of discipleship, therefore, we need to forge a method as practical and down-to-earth as the *General Rules*, and as accountable as the early class meeting. This will not be difficult, for we need only do what our forebears did: Go back to the teachings of Jesus. What may prove difficult for a church as self-indulgent as we have become, however, is actually to put the method into practice.

For Thought and Discussion

1. What do you understand by "traditioning" the class meeting?

2. Wesley's *General Rules* stated that Methodists were those who, "having the form" were "seeking the power of godliness" (p. 62). Is that how you understand your own Christian discipleship?

3. What is the teaching that Wesley described as "devilish"? (p. 64). Do you agree with him?

4. Do you "work for your spiritual food"? (page 65).

5. In what ways do you think the "method" of the early Methodists can help us in our discipleship today?

6. On page 69, the format of the class meeting is likened to that of Alcoholics Anonymous or Weight Watchers. Discuss.

7. Discuss the language of the 1780 *Collection of Hymns* (page 70). Have you ever known a "backslider"? Have you ever been one yourself?

8. "Christians should be suspicious, therefore, of any activity which suggests that a retreat from the world is the way to God" (page 73). Discuss.

Chapter 5

The General Rule of Discipleship

It has been the premise of our study thus far that the early Methodist class meeting is one of the best models we have for Christian discipleship today. As we have examined this "excellent institution," we have found it to be simple, yet demanding. We have noted that the class meeting was by no means merely a time of sharing, but a form of mutual accountability. The richness of Christian fellowship which the members experienced week by week came as a blessing; but this was not the purpose for which these early Methodists gathered. Their concern was first and foremost to keep close to their set course—to walk with Jesus Christ in the world and to serve him faithfully in preparing for the coming reign of God.

We also noted that this weekly accountability had two basic criteria: an account of each member's spiritual well-being and an account of each one's compliance with the *General Rules* of the societies. In this way, the members were accountable for both the power and the form of their discipleship. Their privileges (spiritual communion with God) did not subsume their obligations (serving Jesus Christ in the world).

MERCY AND PIETY: SOCIAL AND PERSONAL

Wesley's *General Rules* are still a reliable set of guidelines for Christian discipleship. They not only place a complementary emphasis on works of mercy and works of piety—the two dimensions of the Christian life that must always be kept in tension—but they also provide a healthy correlation between public and private disciplines—the social and the personal.

This balanced emphasis on works of mercy and piety in their social and personal dimensions provides a solid foundation for discipleship in our own day and age. We need to change Wesley's language, of course, because *mercy* and *piety* have different connotations today, as do *public* and *private*. Moreover, we are now living in a post-Marxian and post-Freudian age, with some insights into human history, human society, and human behavior that are very different from those of the eighteenth century.

A NEW GENERAL RULE

Allowing for these contextual changes, it is possible to find terms that usefully and appropriately translate the main principles of Wesley's *General Rules*. Thus, works of mercy in their personal and social forms can be translated today into "acts of compassion" and "acts of justice," both of which are necessary in the Christian life. By the same token, works of piety can be translated into public "acts of worship" and private "acts of devotion." Again, both are necessary in the Christian life. Held together in a healthy tension, these can be formulated as a new "General Rule of Discipleship" for the church of today:

To witness to Jesus Christ in the world,
and to follow his teachings through
acts of compassion, justice, worship, and devotion,
under the guidance of the Holy Spirit.

[WORKS OF MERCY]

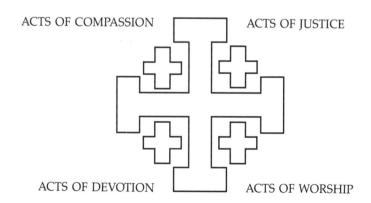

ACTS OF COMPASSION   ACTS OF JUSTICE

ACTS OF DEVOTION   ACTS OF WORSHIP

[WORKS OF PIETY]

A FOURFOLD TENSION

Those who are familiar with the Wesleyan theological method of "Scripture, Tradition, Reason, and Experience" will find it interesting that this new General Rule likewise comprises a quadrilateral. The advantage of its fourfold approach to discipleship is much the same as that of the fourfold theological method—it helps us to avoid imbalance. By keeping all four dimensions of our discipleship in a healthy tension, we are less likely to fall into one of the most subtle errors of the Christian life—playing to our strengths, or worse, to our preferences.

This has been a perennial pitfall for Christian disciples across the history of the church and, ironically, the reason we stumble into it so often is the assurance that comes from following Jesus Christ. When we are reconciled to God in Christ and come to know the indwelling Holy Spirit, there is a sense of God's presence which overwhelms us. Indeed, so fully does this assurance fill our lives that it is easy to forget we are embarked on a spiritual journey, with a great deal of sinful resistance still to be overcome, both in us and around us. The temptation is to stay where we are, enjoying our spiritual benefits, but all the while neglecting our obligations.

Therein lies the error and the self-deception: We assume that whatever feels good, appears attractive, or is relatively easy to accomplish, is what constitutes our Christian discipleship. Some of the time this will be the case, but by no means always—as the words of John Wesley's *Covenant Service* pointedly illustrate:

> Christ has many services to be done. Some are more easy and honourable, others more difficult and disgraceful. Some are suitable to our inclinations and interests, others are contrary to both. In some we may please Christ and please ourselves. . . . But then there are other works, wherein we cannot please Christ, but by denying ourselves.[36]

A BASIC CHECKLIST

The extent to which we deceive ourselves in this regard can best be revealed by running through a basic checklist, such as Wesley's *General Rules* or the new General Rule of Discipleship. This is not to suggest that Christian discipleship can be reduced to a set of regulations; still less is it to exclude the spiritual promptings which, as we have already noted, call faithful disciples to special service for Christ at particular times and places. But it is to give our discipleship a reliable *shape*, a balanced *form*.

Airline pilots, for example, know that every flight will be different, with all sorts of unpredictable factors, such as weather, mechanical performance, and passenger load. Yet there are certain basics which govern every flight, and pilots perform standard checks accordingly. By the same token, the birth of every child is different, as any mother can verify, again with all sorts of unpredictable factors. Yet there are certain stages through which every birth proceeds, with standard checks for the doctors and nurses in attendance.

AN OLD MISTAKE

The fact that so few Christians today are willing to accept even the need for checks and balances in their discipleship is a sure sign that we have fallen into the very trap we have just identified—the assumption that our freedom in Christ dispenses with the need for any basic guidelines. The mistake is an old one, and the technical word for it is *antinomianism*, which literally means "against the law." We know it was a danger for our early Methodist forebears no less than for ourselves, because Wesley's preaching, especially after 1750, increasingly focused on the importance of the Old Testament as well as the New. He stressed the need to observe the law of God, not dispense with it. Christ was to be proclaimed as prophet no less than priest.[37]

CHRISTIAN LICENSE

When we neglect the laws of God, which Jesus specifically declared he had come to fulfill, not to abolish (Matt. 5:17), we do not exercise Christian freedom. We rather indulge in Christian license—the self-serving and supremely pompous assertion that we are now infallibly guided by the Holy Spirit. This means that we can do exactly what we wish, provided "our hearts be free to it" (i.e., that we feel good about it).[38]

Would that we could be so sure about our ability to discern

God's will! In point of fact, we are far from infallible in this area. But instead of accepting this as a given of the Christian life, we often become obsessed with trying to rationalize it. As a result, we find ourselves dwelling on the theological or spiritual issue of whether God's guidance is trustworthy, when the real question is much more practical and obvious—whether we are trustworthy servants.

Our failure to deal with this question is in large measure the reason for our neglect of the teachings of Jesus. Indeed, things have reached the point today where faithful disciples hesitate to correct one another. Not being able to discern the will of God to our spiritual satisfaction, we disdain the basic guidelines for discipleship which Jesus left us, and concede the directions for our daily living in the world to the abstractions of social principles or the pronouncements of religious experts.

Authentic Christian disciples, by contrast, accept the need for both the power and the form of God's grace. They affirm the indwelling Holy Spirit who empowers them "both to will and to work" for God's good pleasure (Phil. 2:13). But they also affirm the teachings of Jesus as the form of their discipleship, and declare that they will do their best to practice them. The need today is not for spiritual overachievers, nor yet for Christic cybernetics, but merely for faithful disciples who will unabashedly witness to Jesus Christ in the world and endeavor to obey his standing orders.

THE GENERAL RULE OF DISCIPLESHIP

This call to faithful discipleship was at the heart of Wesley's evangelical message in the eighteenth century, and his *General Rules* of 1743 are a clear indication of how the early Methodists responded and shaped their live accordingly. As we have suggested in the preceding chapters, the same call to discipleship is needed today; and with the call must likewise come a clear indication of how faithful disciples can shape their lives after Jesus of Nazareth in the contemporary world.

This is precisely the purpose of the new General Rule of Discipleship: "To witness to Jesus Christ in the world, and to follow his teachings through acts of compassion, justice, worship, and devotion, under the guidance of the Holy Spirit." Drawing on the early Methodist *Rules* and on the theological principles of John Wesley, the General Rule is designed to provide faithful disciples with a simple and straightforward method for Christian living in the world. For this, as we have already noted, we need both form and power. Without the power of God's grace, our discipleship becomes a mere formality. Without the form of God's law, our discipleship becomes self-indulgent. Accordingly, the General Rule directs us to follow the teachings of Jesus (form) under the guidance of the Holy Spirit (power); and we shall now examine these directives in some detail.

WITNESSING TO JESUS CHRIST

Implicit throughout Wesley's *General Rules* is the cardinal privilege and duty of Christian discipleship: witnessing to Jesus Christ. Unfortunately, in our day and age this can no longer be implicit; it must be made very explicit indeed. Whereas vital Christian witness used to be normative in the early days of Methodism, today it has become more of an exception. In church-wide planning and strategy it is often taken for granted; and in local congregations it is often supplanted by myriad ministries, which do everything, it seems, except give honor to the Christ in whose name and for whose glory the church exists.

Fortunately, there are many parts of the Methodist church worldwide where witnessing to Jesus Christ—proclaiming him as prophet and redeemer, and calling on all people to acknowledge him as sovereign of the coming reign of God—is still at the heart of Christian discipleship. But in the United States of America this is by no means always the case. Being a Christian in this country is all too often a merely cultural identification, with little knowledge of God's radical justice in Jesus of Nazareth, crucified, dead, and buried, or of God's radical grace in Jesus the Christ, raised from the dead, ascended into heaven, and soon to come again.

Accordingly, the new General Rule begins with a firm directive to Christian disciples: Make clear *whose* teachings you endeavor to follow. Jesus was quite unambiguous about his expectations in this regard: "Those who are ashamed of me and of my words, of them the Son of Man will be ashamed when he comes in his glory and the glory of the Father and of the holy angels" (Luke 9:26).

WITNESSING IN THE WORLD

It may seem redundant to add emphasis with this further phrase to the opening directive of the General Rule. Surely any witness to Jesus Christ is bound to be "in the world." Is that not where we find ourselves most of the time? Indeed, is that not where we live out our lives?

We noted earlier that worldly Christian living was the genius of Wesley's spiritual leadership. He did not attempt to take the Methodist societies out of the world, but instead showed them how to follow God in the rough and tumble of daily living. This was also the purpose of his preaching in the open air. When taken to task by those who complained that there were plenty of churches for people to attend, he pointed out that his mission was to reach the people who would not come to church, but who *would* come to hear him in the fields.[39]

Since Wesley's day, however, Methodism has become established as a church—indeed, as a number of denominations. Like the Church of England in Wesley's day, we too have plenty of churches for people to attend; and our concern, our overwhelming concern, is how to get them filled. Such is our concern, in fact, that we have come to spend a great part of our lives in our churches, hoping that others will join us.

As a result, many of us do not have the time, or do not see the need, to witness to Christ in the world. We witness instead to one another, if we witness at all. The General Rule therefore directs faithful Christian disciples to reach out beyond their church communities, and to let all the world know the good news of the gospel of Jesus Christ.

FOLLOWING THE TEACHINGS OF JESUS

The next directive of the General Rule is to follow the teachings of Jesus through acts of compassion, justice, worship, and devotion. We shall deal with each of these areas in turn; but first, we would do well to remember the method by which our early Methodist forebears practiced their discipleship. They attended a weekly class meeting to hold themselves mutually accountable for their spiritual walk with Christ and for their obedience to his commands.

In these four dimensions of the General Rule, therefore, faithful disciples must not only strive to follow the teachings of Jesus. They must also be ready to hold themselves accountable for doing so.

ACCOUNTABILITY FOR ACTS OF COMPASSION

Acts of compassion come under the category of what Wesley called "works of mercy"; and it is noteworthy that in the *General Rules* he lists the works of mercy before the works of piety. This would appear to give his evangelical critics good ammunition for their charge of "works-righteousness"; yet it is merely another example of the common sense with which he led the Methodist societies. For the truth of the matter is that while our faith in Christ is very much a variable, subject to our temperaments, our circumstances, and even our moods, our service for Christ is not subject to these variables at all—or it most certainly should not be. The hungry need feeding, whether or not we are in the mood. The naked need to be clothed, whether or not it is convenient for us. The sick need help, whether or not we are feeling up to it. And those in prison need to be visited, whether or not we feel we have very much to offer them.

Common Courtesies

In other words, basic acts of compassion can and should be performed by anyone at any time. They do not require the services of a super-saint. That is why Wesley lists them in the *General Rules* ahead of the means of grace; and it is also why they are listed as the first of Christ's teachings in the new General Rule. The significance of this becomes clear when we consider how often those of us with strong faith neglect to incorporate such simple, basic acts of kindness into our lifestyle; and how often these same acts are performed on a regular basis by those who feel inferior when it comes to talking about their faith. The directive of the General Rule is unavoidable: We should all look around, find out who is in need, and then do something about it.

ACCOUNTABILITY FOR ACTS OF JUSTICE

Once we do look around us and discover who is in need, the General Rule points us toward another important dimension of Christian discipleship: acts of justice. This exposes even more clearly the blind spot to which we alluded a moment ago, namely our tendency in the church to focus on the New Testament to the neglect of the Old—which is profoundly to misunderstand the teachings of Jesus, who was steeped in the Hebrew scriptures. It is also to misunderstand the nature of God, whose dealings with the people of Israel throughout their history show that divine righteousness and justice are no less powerful than divine love.

God's justice is not a legalistic righteousness, however, nor is it impartial. Contrary to the Greek and Roman concepts of morality and law which are often inferred from the language of the New Testament, the righteousness of God which we find in the teachings of Jesus is grounded in the long encounter between Yahweh and the Hebrews. It has a strongly personal quality, and echoes the Old Testament prophets, such as Amos, Hosea, and Micah. Most important of all, it is weighted toward the poor and the helpless.

Justice with an Agenda

The justice of God is justice with an agenda, the agenda of a God who is deeply offended by those who take advantage of the widow and the orphan, and those who exercise power irresponsibly. It is the same agenda which Jesus announced in the Nazareth synagogue when he read from the scroll (Isa. 61:1-2; Luke 4:18-19), and which he affirmed in the Sermon on the Mount when he proclaimed that he had not come to abolish the law and the prophets, but to fulfill them (Matt. 5:17). Those who are disciples of Jesus must take heed and do no less.

Alongside acts of compassion, therefore, we must perform acts of justice. We must not only meet people's needs, but ask why they are in need in the first place. Some of this will happen as a matter of course, because once we get involved with the poor and the needy, we see with new eyes the social systems that victimize them, and are compelled to enter into their struggles.

Social Risk

There are other issues we need to address, however, primarily because they are an offense to the God whose law was thundered from Sinai. This may well entail political involvements, and will almost certainly incur the risk of taking stands that are controversial. Moreover, there is no guarantee that we will always be correct in this dimension of our discipleship. We know for certain how to minister to hungry persons: As an act of compassion, we give them food. It is usually much less clear, however, what we should do to address the reasons for their hunger. The issues are rarely cut and dried, and there are almost always multiple options and differing points of view.

Mutual Consultation

This is where the model of early Methodist discipleship once again proves to be practical and down-to-earth. Not only does the General Rule complement our acts of justice with compassion, worship, and devotion, thereby ensuring that the enormity of social and global injustice does not overwhelm us; but also, by following the Wesleyan method of mutual accountability, we are assured of support and advice from reliable colleagues—mutual consultation on a regular basis with fellow Christian disciples of like mind and purpose. Many times this consultation (what Wesley described as "Christian conference") will open new possibilities for our witness in the world. And even if we feel prompted to act against their advice, at least we have the assurance of knowing that our prompting has been well and truly tested.

Social Responsibility

If mutual consultation such as this were to be a regular feature of our congregational life and work, the social witness of the church at large would surely be more informed and more responsible. On the one hand, those charged with shaping our prophetic ministries would have the best possible sources for their data—the people who are living out the gospel on a day-to-day basis across the land. On the other hand, local congregations would discover what it is like to accept responsibility for prophetic ministry, right where they live and work. They would experience the immediacy of walking with the Jew from Nazareth, and weathering the opposition he encountered as well as the adulation. For that matter, they would also experience what it was like to join the early Methodists, who also had their share of opposition.

ACCOUNTABILITY FOR ACTS OF WORSHIP

When we come to the works of piety in Wesley's *General Rules,* it is interesting to note that the public, or corporate, means of grace precede those which are personal. Public worship—the ministry of the Word and the Supper of the Lord—come before the disciplines of private prayer, searching the scriptures, and fasting, or abstinence. Apart from the fact that this affirms the indispensable place of the church in Christian discipleship, it is yet one more example of the common sense of Wesley's *Rules.* Our private devotional disciplines will often founder on our doubts and uncertainties. When we worship together, however, we "watch over one another in love" and "build each other up" in the Body of Christ.

Liturgical Renewal

Accordingly, acts of worship precede acts of devotion in the new General Rule; and in terms of being accountable for acts of worship, we have a tremendous advantage today. We are living at a time of rich liturgical renewal. The new *Hymnal* of The United Methodist Church is proving to be a treasure house of Christian tradition, in words and music both.[40] Theology is being impacted by worship, as in Geoffrey Wainwright's classic volume *Doxology.*[41] Preaching is once again high on the agenda of theological education. The sacraments are being given renewed prominence as a true means of grace. Most important of all, congregations are finding the hour of worship to be the focal point of their life and work, when Christ can be honored as at no other time of the week.

To Glorify God

Yet the General Rule cautions us at this point. Yes, it is good that our worship, our preaching, and our sacramental life are being renewed. But as part of an accountable discipleship, we must take care not to measure this renewal solely or even primarily by the level of satisfaction of those who participate. The chief purpose of acts of worship is to glorify God, and in so doing to open ourselves to grace. The regularity of worship, therefore, both in word and sacrament, is far more important than the benefits we derive from them. Not that the benefits are unimportant; nor are they the priority. As with so much else in our discipleship, it is a case of putting the horse before the cart.

A Personal Illustration

This was a lesson I learned some years ago when I became friends with a vicar, or parish priest, of the Church of England. One evening he invited me to supper in his 300-year-old rectory adjoining the 400-year-old parish church. Before we sat down to eat, he asked me if I would like to attend Evensong; and of course I accepted. We walked over to the church at ten minutes of six; at five minutes of six he rang the bell vigorously (he was a very large and fit vicar!); at two minutes of six we sat down in the chancel, he on one side and I on the other. No one else came, but at six o'clock we began the service. He led and I responded.

On our return to the rectory, I was curious. "How often do you hold Evensong?" I asked.

"Each evening, Monday through Friday."

I was even more curious. "Is this your average evening congregation?"

"No, it's double, actually."

I was now incredulous. "You mean that each evening you say Evensong to yourself?"

"No, not at all. First, I do not say it to myself. God is worshiped. Second, people in the village hear the bell, and know that the church is on the job. Third, it's in the *Discipline*."

His words have stayed with me over the years, and it has often occurred to me since then that the most underused part of many of our church premises today is the sanctuary. We are free to worship, whenever we wish, however we wish. Yet most days of the week, the place we have set apart as sacred space for this tremendous earthly privilege remains empty. How thoughtlessly we abuse the privileges of our religious freedom!

ACCOUNTABILITY FOR ACTS OF DEVOTION

The General Rule concludes the teachings of Jesus with an accountability for personal devotions. In many ways, this is the most difficult part of Christian discipleship, for it is the time when we enter into the presence of God directly.

Of course, we have encountered God in our acts of compassion. We have joined Christ among the homeless, among the drug addicts, and among the abused, rejected castoffs of society. And more, we have been privileged to know that in reaching out to persons such as these, we have not only joined with Christ; we have ministered to him in the power and presence of the Holy Spirit.

Likewise in our acts of justice, we have joined with the prophet from Nazareth, confronting, in the name of the God of righteousness, the powers and principalities of this world. And more, we have been privileged on occasion to see the Holy Spirit bring justice, to see the sinned-against of the world achieve new dignity and worth as children of God.

In our acts of worship we have also encountered the risen Christ, present in the Holy Spirit. And more, at moments of high privilege, we have beheld God's glory, full of grace and truth (John 1:14). We have tasted the firstfruits of our resurrection in Christ (1 Cor. 15:20).

Face to Face with God

All of this notwithstanding, the times when we come face to face with God most directly are in those disciplines of private devotion—prayer, meditation, and searching the scriptures—when no one else is present, and our conversation with God is intensely personal. The other dimensions of the General Rule are by no means irrelevant to such times, because they ensure that we do not deceive ourselves by merely projecting our own desires onto what is properly a dialogue with God. But we must never allow our other works of discipleship to substitute for private devotions. Self-deception is a very real possibility in the busyness of compassion, justice, and worship. If these activities deprive us of our personal relationship with God, something is seriously wrong.

We should not be overwhelmed by the sense of the holy which surrounds the devotional task. We have Jesus of Nazareth as our role model, and we have as our mentors that "great cloud of witnesses" who have run their race and are now cheering us on (Heb. 12:1-2)—not least of whom are the forebears we have encountered at many stages in our study of the Methodist tradition. Nor do we need to attempt these acts of devotion in a vacuum. There is a wealth of literature on prayer; there are numerous aids for personal Bible study; and there are many devotional guides available, often with an accompanying daily plan to follow.[42]

Even so, the final decision will always rest with us. We are the ones who will ultimately be responsible for developing the disciplines of prayer, Bible study, and personal reflection. We should be under no illusions in this regard: It will be a *work* of piety. Our acts of devotion will entail effort and application; and we will not become disciplined without much practice.

Alone with God

These are the disciplines, however, which will ultimately refine us as Christian disciples. For it is in those moments of quietness, when there is nowhere to hide and nothing to distract, that God will deal with us most personally, and shape our discipleship most directly. The great spiritual writer Oswald Chambers puts it this way:

> We have to get rid of the idea that we understand ourselves. It is the last conceit to go. The only One who understands us is God. . . . There are whole tracts of stubbornness and ignorance to be revealed by the Holy Spirit in each one of us, and it can only be done when Jesus gets us alone.[43]

THE DISCIPLINE OF FASTING

There is one area of accountability, identified in Wesley's *General Rules* as an instituted means of grace, but difficult to categorize within the new General Rule; and that is fasting, or abstinence. It is difficult to place primarily because of our obsession in the Western world with physical and emotional well-being. What used to be a spiritual discipline or a sacrificial act in the eighteenth century is all too often regarded today as a means of personal fulfillment, or even as a fad.

We shall discuss this in more detail in chapter six. Suffice it for now to say that the care of our bodies—mentally, emotionally, and physically—is no less an aspect of our discipleship than any other. And it most certainly qualifies as a "work" of piety in our own day and age because of the pressures under which so many of us have to determine our personal priorities.

ACCOUNTABILITY TO THE HOLY SPIRIT

When we have exercised accountability for all of these works of discipleship, the General Rule directs us to accountability for obedience to the Holy Spirit. If we are to appropriate the early class meeting for today, we need to understand this deepest truth of all about the weekly meetings. Whenever Christian disciples meet together in the name of Christ, they will not only watch over one another in love. Something else will happen. The Spirit of God will be present, working in and through the dynamics of the group, to empower them for service in preparing for the coming reign of God, on earth as in heaven.

THE THREAT OF CHRIST'S PRESENCE

This is why Christian disciples the world over are drawn to such fellowship as the source of their spiritual strength. It is not only a scriptural promise that Christ will be in the midst of those who gather in his name—a promise claimed and honored in the richness of *koinonia* from the earliest days of the church. It is also something of a threat. Christ *will* be present on those occasions, and the Holy Spirit *will* have promptings and warnings for which faithful disciples must be prepared, and which they must be ready to obey.

In the sharing of their spiritual insights—discouragements and defeats, joys and victories, strengths and weaknesses, burdens of injustice and hopes of God's liberating righteousness—Christian disciples find the bedrock of their faith. And at each stage of their journey, they find the grace of God more sustaining, as they lose themselves more profoundly in the will of God.

PROMPTINGS AND WARNINGS OF THE HOLY SPIRIT

Learning how to recognize these spiritual promptings and warnings is one of the most important dimensions of a mutually accountable discipleship; and in large measure it simply means using the right language. For example, Christian disciples do not have "bright ideas"; they have "promptings" or "nudgings" from the Holy Spirit. By the same token, Christian disciples do not have "twinges of conscience"; they have "warnings" from the Holy Spirit. Identifying these warnings and promptings sharpens the discernment of faithful disciples. To go further and to share them with one another means a quantum leap forward in their spiritual life, for their discernments and learnings are thereby greatly multiplied.

ACCOUNTABILITY TO AND FOR THE CHURCH

All of this brings us back to the central challenge of the class meeting for the church of today: *ecclesiola in ecclesia*. First, we must be reminded one more time of the very significant change that has taken place since the time of the early Methodist societies. Methodism has become a church, at once inclusive and pluralistic. In a very real sense, The United Methodist Church is now the equivalent of the Church of England in Wesley's day. We should therefore expect small groups to emerge in varying forms and with varying purposes, just as they did in the eighteenth century. We should acknowledge and affirm these various *ecclesiolae*, or "little churches," and endeavor to keep them *in ecclesia*, in the "big church," as a means of grace and enrichment for our ministry and mission.

THE FEW AND THE MANY

We must then remember the accountable discipleship of the class meeting, and our premise that there are Christians today, no less than in Wesley's day, who are ready to accept such a call—who are ready to fulfill their discipleship through a method of mutual accountability. We must also remember that there are those whose pilgrimage in the Christian faith has not yet brought them to this point, and who come to church primarily to be fed, and healed, and taught, and loved.

The challenge which faces us, therefore, is how to be accepting of both the few and the many in the life and work of the congregation: how to nurture a large, inclusive church, but at the same time acknowledge the accountable disciples for who they really are—mentors in the faith.

CONGREGATIONAL LEADERSHIP

In other words, the most important lesson we can learn from the early class meeting is in the area of congregational leadership. If we accept that an accountable disciple is a role model for the Christian life, then congregational leadership takes on a whole new shape. Instead of being entrusted to "professional" staff with appropriate programmatic "skills," leadership becomes a dynamic fusion of the particular gifts and graces of accountable disciples, clergy and laity alike.

The distinction which then emerges is not between "skilled" and "unskilled" leaders, but rather between those who are ready to be held accountable for their discipleship and those who are not. The question is not who has gifts and graces, but who is prepared to *use* them. It is not a matter of training, but of *commitment*. Exhortation is not the watchword, but *example*.

The prevailing view of pastoral leadership in the church has blurred this distinction, with the result that many clergy are over-burdened with tasks they were never meant to handle, and many laypersons who are ready to assume leadership roles are denied the opportunity. But once the leadership of congregations is de-fined in terms of *accountability* for discipleship, it becomes clear that we must draw the distinction afresh.

COVENANT DISCIPLESHIP GROUPS

It is precisely this sort of leadership which covenant discipleship groups are designed to foster, and it is time now to describe their nature and their function. As we do so, many similarities to the early class meeting will become apparent, along with some significant differences.

Covenant discipleship groups are designed on the one hand to affirm the validity of the *ecclesia*, the big church, with all of its structures and teachings, and on the other hand to embody a particular form of the *ecclesiola*, the little church. They do not preclude other forms of *ecclesiola* in the life and work of the church; on the contrary, they often strengthen them with enhanced leadership and participation. But they do have a very particular function. They focus on the one dimension of the class meeting we do not have today: a mutual accountability for the basics of Christian living in the world. Shaped by the General Rule of Discipleship, they will hopefully draw together the "methodical" disciples of today.

HOLDING FAST

As Wesley made clear to us more than 200 years ago, Christian discipleship is rarely experienced as spiritual growth, even though growth does take place and is to be expected. Faithful discipleship, lived out in the power of the Holy Spirit according to the guidelines of Jesus Christ, is much more a matter of *holding fast*. It is doing the best we can with the gifts we have received, in the freedom and responsibility of joyful obedience.

Covenant discipleship groups are for those who wish to share in that commitment, so that the church as a whole can more effectively serve Jesus of Nazareth, the one who has been named to preside over the coming reign of God.

For Thought and Discussion

1. Do you find the General Rule of Discipleship a helpful updating of Wesley's *General Rules?*

2. Do you find any examples of "antinomianism" in the church of today? (p. 80)

3. Small groups are widespread in the contemporary North American church. In light of the General Rule of Discipleship, should any of these groups be re-examined for their true purpose?

4. Do you agree that God's justice has an agenda? (p. 85)

5. Do you agree that "mutual consultation" could make the social witness of the church "more informed and more responsible"? (p. 86)

6. What lesson do you draw from the personal illustration about worship on page 88?

7. "We have to get rid of the idea that we understand ourselves. It is the last conceit to go" (Oswald Chambers, quoted on page 90). Discuss.

8. Do you agree that "accountable disciples" rather than "professional staff" are the appropriate leaders for local congregations? (pages 93-94)

Chapter 6

Forming a
Covenant Discipleship Group

*A covenant discipleship group consists of two to
seven people who agree to meet together for one
hour per week in order to hold themselves mutually
accountable for their discipleship. They do this by
affirming a written covenant on which they
themselves have agreed.*

JOINING A GROUP

People usually become members of covenant discipleship groups
in one of four ways:

1. By joining a pilot group.
Pilot groups meet for a year or more to lead a congregation into
covenant discipleship. They are exactly the same as every other
covenant discipleship group, with one exception: The members
help to form new groups at the end of the pilot year.

2. By responding at a covenant discipleship weekend.
At the conclusion of the pilot year, a special weekend is organized
to introduce the groups to the whole congregation. The focal point
of this is an open invitation during the Sunday morning worship.
Those who respond are organized into new groups, which begin to
meet as soon as days and times can be arranged.

3. By responding to invitations on other occasions.
Once covenant discipleship groups are part of the life and work of a
congregation, they remain open to new members at any time.
Invitations to join are extended throughout the year, such as on

Covenant Sunday, at any worship service, and by special presentations to Sunday school classes or other church activities.

4. By visiting a group.

Prospective members are welcome to attend covenant discipleship meetings, either at their own request, or by the invitation of a member. The only stipulation is that the number of such visits is limited to three, following which a decision must be made whether or not to join.

GROUP MEMBERSHIP

Covenant discipleship groups function without any membership restrictions concerning age, sex, or marital status. For contextual reasons, a group may be made up of men or women only, but the great majority have mixed membership, since the mutual accountability of discipleship applies to all persons alike. Some married couples, for example, prefer to join the same group; others prefer to be in separate groups. Some families wish to be in a group together; in other instances, young people prefer to be in covenant apart from their parents.

COVENANT DISCIPLESHIP FOR YOUNG PEOPLE

While there are no hard and fast rules about the age range of covenant discipleship groups, there are occasions when young people find themselves in Christian community away from their families. This happens to some extent in congregations and in high schools; it happens much more on college campuses.

To respond to these particular situations, two resources have been adapted from covenant discipleship; for youth in congregations, and for young people on college campuses. One is *Branch Groups: Covenant Discipleship for Youth*, by Lisa Grant (Available thru Covenant Discipleship). The other is *Covenants on Campus: Covenant Discipleship Groups for College and University Students*, by Kim A. Hauenstein-Mallet and Kenda Creasy Dean (Discipleship Resources, 1991, order no. DR099). Details of these and other Discipleship Resources publications can be found in the Resources listing on p. 171.

COVENANT DISCIPLESHIP AT SEMINARY

Christian formation is increasingly a feature of student life at seminaries, divinity schools, and schools of theology. At a number of these schools, covenant discipleship groups are either part of the curriculum, or a voluntary student activity. They function in the same way as in congregations, though, for obvious reasons, they meet only through the academic year and re-group each fall and spring.

THE NUMBER OF MEMBERS

The maximum number of members recommended for a covenant discipleship group is seven. The only reason for this is logistics. If a group is to be held accountable for a covenant which may have ten clauses or more, it is difficult to involve more than seven people in one hour. Since the one strict rule of covenant discipleship is that the meetings last no more than an hour, the size of the group must be limited accordingly.

On the other hand, there is no minimum number for a group. A few groups have worked very effectively with three, or even two members. By and large, however, it has been found that when groups have fewer than four members, the dynamic of the meeting is impeded. Absences are felt more acutely, and there is less diversity of Christian discipleship. In practice, the average covenant discipleship group numbers five or six, leaving room for new members to join, yet also leaving a good group on those occasions when not everyone can be present.

If a sizeable number of the members have work which frequently takes them out of town, groups may extend their membership to eight or ten, with the expectancy that one or two will always be absent. Again, there are no hard and fast rules. Each group plans its own logistics.

THE RIGHT DAY AND TIME

No matter how people come to join a covenant discipleship group, only one thing will determine which group they join: convenience of schedule. Just as there are no restrictions as to whether a person is married or single, or whether a married couple or family members belong to the same or different groups, no determination is made on grounds of faith, background, or personality. The only question a prospective member needs to ask about a covenant discipleship group is, What day and time does it meet? By the same token, the only question to be asked of a prospective member is, Can you make this day and time a priority in your weekly schedule?

TASK ORIENTED

For those who have some experience of small groups, organizing covenant discipleship groups solely by day and time seems to be a haphazard, if not foolhardy, method of proceeding. The dynamics of a group, it is argued, depend to a large degree on the ability of the members to relate to one another and to be sensitive to each other's needs. If there is not some basic compatibility, therefore, the interpersonal sharing of the group is unlikely to be effective.

Yet it is precisely this factor which makes a covenant discipleship group different from most other small groups that function in church settings. Covenant discipleship groups are not for interpersonal sharing, though sharing takes place. They are structured rather for *mutual accountability*. The people who make this commitment do so for a clear purpose: to develop consistency and maturity in their walk with Christ.

In other words, covenant discipleship groups are *task-oriented*. And because they are task-oriented, it matters very little what kind of persons make up their membership. They come together first and foremost to help each other become better Christian disciples. How they relate to one another, therefore, is much less important than how they relate to Christ.

WHAT COVENANT DISCIPLESHIP
GROUPS ARE NOT

To make this point clear, it might be helpful to state what covenant discipleship groups are not. They are certainly not encounter groups. Nor are they any number of other kinds of small groups often found in church settings. For example, they are not Bible study groups; they are not prayer groups; they are not growth groups; they are not spiritual formation groups; they are not advocacy groups; they are not service groups; and they are not care groups or share groups. All of these aspects of Christian discipleship and community will feature in covenant discipleship groups, over and over again; but none of them is the purpose of their weekly meetings.

Covenant discipleship groups are nothing more than a weekly checkpoint of accountability, and nothing less. Judge Merrill Hartman of Dallas has summed them up very well: "My covenant discipleship group is not where my discipleship happens. It's where I make *sure* that it does."

THE TOP PRIORITY: BE THERE

The most important rule for covenant discipleship group members is thus quite simple: *Be there!*

Once you have joined a covenant discipleship group, begin right away to arrange your calendar. Avoid scheduling meetings or events that conflict with this weekly appointment. Begin to think of your attendance at the group as one of your basic routines—something you do as a matter of course, unless there is an emergency or you are away from home. It is surprising how seldom you need to be absent once you prioritize this time.

Likewise, make it a priority to let someone in the group know if you cannot attend. Surprise absences make it difficult for the others to "watch over you in love," and you also place a burden on the mutual trust of the group. If your absence is unavoidable, try to link up with the group in some way. For example, you might be able to talk by telephone for a few minutes while the group is meeting. Alternatively, you may be able to pause for prayer wherever you are at the time, thus joining with the others in spirit.

Of course, when you return, be ready to give an account of your discipleship for the time you were away, as well as for the past week.

THE IMPORTANCE OF REGULAR ATTENDANCE

The importance of regular attendance will become clear as the life and work of your covenant discipleship group develop. But there are four good reasons for making it such a priority:

1. We are in covenant with God.

The biblical word for *covenant* signifies an agreement that is non-negotiable once it is made. When we enter into a covenant with God, we bind ourselves to a contract which we cannot undo later, even if it proves inconvenient. All we can do is to break it.

2. We are in covenant with each other.

In a covenant discipleship group, we also make a covenant with each other, which is just as binding as the covenant we have with God. And the most important part of the covenant is that we agree to meet weekly. This much we can always manage to do, never mind how well or how badly we have fared with the other dimensions of our Christian discipleship.

3. There is no pressure to "succeed."

If everyone in the group is firmly committed to being there each week, a tremendous pressure is removed. No person is under any obligation to "make things happen." No one has to make the group meeting "successful" or "meaningful." Everyone can relax in the sure knowledge that the group does not have to "prove itself" to anyone, least of all to its own members.

4. You can come "just as you are."

Just as this removes pressure from the group, it also removes pressure from each member. It means that you do not have to "get into the right mood" for your covenant discipleship meeting. Nor do you have to "get something out of it." You agree to be there, whatever your feelings, whatever your expectations. In other words, you can always come "just as you are."

CERTAINTY IN THE MIDST OF UNCERTAINTIES

In the midst of so many uncertainties in human relationships today—dishonest promises, broken agreements, family disintegrations, demands for instant satisfaction, selfishness masquerading as self-fulfillment, and much, much more—this commitment to be at your weekly meeting, come what may, is one of the most important gifts covenant discipleship group members give to one another.

Just as Christ gave us his assurance that when we gather in his name, he will be there, so we make this the most important rule of covenant discipleship: We too will *be there*. It imparts to each member a deep sense of comfort and assurance; and this in itself is a wondrous means of grace.

TWO MORE "FIRST STEPS"

1. Read this book.

As you begin your weekly meetings, it is helpful to read this book, if you have not already done so. It is not only a guide to covenant discipleship. It is also a grounding of the groups in the Methodist tradition, as well as a collection of comments and advice from covenant discipleship groups that have been meeting for the past fifteen years in the United States and in a number of other countries around the world.

If your group is newly formed, you may want to set aside part of the meeting for a few weeks to reflect on some of the discussion questions following chapters one through five. This will encourage group members to read the book, and thus to have a better idea of the nature and purpose of what they are about. It will also help the group to understand its role in relation to the congregation as a whole—something which is a critical dimension of covenant discipleship groups.

But most important, reading the book will give the members a sense of the tradition of Christian small groups out of which covenant discipleship was born. In particular, it will direct them toward the early class meeting, perhaps the most distinctive component of the Methodist heritage, and what made the early Methodists "methodical" Christians.

2. Subscribe to the Quarterly.

The *Covenant Discipleship Quarterly* was launched in order to provide continuing resources for covenant discipleship groups, and is now in its sixth year. Each issue carries four regular features:

- *Articles* that deal with important questions for group members, and in particular those dimensions of the gospel which the General Rule of Discipleship brings into focus, impelling us by grace to serve God and our neighbor in the world.

- *Excerpts* from writings in the Christian tradition which show us how faithful servants of Jesus Christ lived out their discipleship in other times and places. In the early issues (still available), the excerpts were drawn primarily from the works of John Wesley. Later issues have included selections from other Methodists, especially the early Methodist preachers, and from spiritual leaders of other traditions. Many of the writings are not readily available elsewhere, and some of the authors are relatively unknown. But all of them have much wisdom to share as we try to follow in their footsteps today.

- *Reports* from covenant discipleship groups across the country, and increasingly across the world, which tell us how God's grace is shaping Christian discipleship in many different contexts. This is probably the most important feature of the *Quarterly*; for if we do not keep ourselves informed of what God is doing through faithful disciples in other places, we are depriving ourselves of a vital means of grace.

  Put differently, if we do not look beyond our own immediate context for the guidance of the Holy Spirit, we are assuming that we have all the ideas, all the answers, and all the spiritual promptings we need—which of course we do not have.

- *Advice* on how to keep your covenant discipleship group faithful to the task in hand—the nuts and bolts of covenant discipleship. You will find samples of group covenants, ideas for recruiting new group members, suggestions for more effective group meetings, and ways in which your group can lead your congregation in Christian discipleship. You will also find announcements of special events, including introductory and advanced workshops in covenant discipleship.

  In addition, from time to time there are *Quarterly Supplements*, which provide resources for particular aspects of the life and work of covenant discipleship groups. These are mailed free of charge to all *Quarterly* subscribers. You can order a subscription to the *Quarterly* by contacting the Covenant Discipleship Office, P. O. Box 840, Nashville, TN 37202, (615)340-7010.

SOME COMMON QUESTIONS

When people make the decision to join a covenant discipleship group, or give it serious thought, it is usually because they have come to see the challenge of being a Christian in a new light, and they want to meet that challenge with the support of other Christians of like mind and purpose.

As with most important decisions, however, they often have some serious second thoughts. If you are in this position, you need to know that you are not alone. Everyone we know of thus far has questions about covenant discipleship groups, both before joining and after. The following are the ones most frequently asked, along with some answers.

Why am I joining a covenant discipleship group?

In the first place, discipleship is not a matter of choice. It is much more a matter of surrender, a giving in to God's gracious initiatives in our lives. We may sing the old hymn, "Have Thine Own Way, Lord," to express our devotion to Christ. But for those of us who have come to this point of surrender, there is a note of desperation when we finally quit resisting, when we finally discover that we cannot follow Christ in our own strength. It is the point at which we realize that we must hand things over to God, bag and baggage: "Very well, God, *have* it your way! One thing's for sure, I can't do it myself any more."

In other words, we enter into Christian discipleship in blind trust, at the end of our tether. We do not know where Christ is going to lead us or what he will ask us to do. All we know is that we have come to a stage where we are willing to take the risk of following him regardless, because all other options have been closed. We may not yet be sure of Jesus Christ, but we have come to be sure of nothing else at all.

It may be that you have come to this point at an early stage in your Christian pilgrimage. If so, you are blessed indeed, for you have found Christian wisdom much sooner than most of us. More likely, however, you made a commitment to Christ some time ago, and have been trying to live a faithful Christian life for many years—and so far, so good. You have been faithful, doing your best to be obedient to the teachings of Jesus, and seeking to walk by the grace of the Holy Spirit.

But now there is another call: "Follow me more closely. I have much more for you to learn and to do. I need your *disciplined* commitment now. Will you take another step with me? Will you trust me even more?"

You have said "yes" to this call, and that is why you are joining a covenant discipleship group.

Does joining a covenant discipleship group mean that my attempts at Christian discipleship thus far have not been good enough?

Not at all. In fact, quite the contrary, or you would not even be hearing this new call, never mind answering it. Everything you have done thus far to be a disciple of Jesus Christ has been commendable: your witness to Christ, at work and in your neighborhood; your regular attendance at church; your faithful participation in a Sunday school class; your involvement in church activities; your attention to Bible study; your regular participation in worship and the sacrament; and your personal devotions of prayer and meditation. All of these have made you a good servant of Jesus Christ.

Likewise you have followed Christ when you have obeyed his commandments to serve God and your neighbor. Perhaps you have been one of those nameless workers who has visited hospitals, ministered to those in prison, staffed the outreach ministries of your church to the poor, and even opened your home to those in need. Or maybe your Christian service has been right in your home, with aging relatives, or problem youngsters, or working at a difficult marriage.

Perhaps your task has been one of social or political action, as you have been gripped by the need to proclaim God's justice to those with secular power—or, just as important, to stand your ground on behalf of those who are too socially disempowered to speak for themselves. Perhaps your mission has been to work for those of our neighbors whom we never know in person, but whose voices reach us from the places of oppression in the world—or worse, whose voices have been silenced by hunger, imprisonment, or death.

If so, your name may never be written large in the annals of churchly recognition. But you will be joining the saints whom we honor for their advancement of the kingdom, the coming new age of Jesus Christ.

In all of this, you have looked to God for guidance, done the best you can, and in turn, been given grace for the task in hand.

Then why do I feel the need to go further by joining a covenant discipleship group?

The first reason we have dealt with already: You are being called by the Spirit of God to take a new step in your discipleship.

But there is another reason, and it has to do with our *maturity* as Christian disciples. The more we follow Christ, the more we grow in grace. As with all real growth, it takes place when we are not aware of it—until, that is, something happens to let us know that we have changed.

Such experiences are common in other areas of growth. For example, we can all remember as a child finding that we could reach a high shelf that used to be too high; or on getting to middle age, discovering that our clothes have "shrunk." We remember what it was like to have someone share a problem with us for the first time, thereby letting us know we were trustworthy; or to be taken seriously in a conversation by an older person, thereby having our point of view respected for the first time. We never quite know when and how we grow to these occasions; but when they happen, we know we have changed.

In our growth as Christian disciples, however, there is a paradox. The more we grow in grace, the more we discover our lack of growth. The more we walk with Christ, the more we realize how much we lack the strength merely to keep pace. Our growth as Christian disciples is not so much a matter of achievement as of learning how to hold fast, how to stay the course.

This is why it usually takes us some time to acquire maturity in our discipleship. At first we tend to devote ourselves to Christ with all of our own energies—and these are not inconsiderable. But gradually we find that the only way to *sustain* Christian discipleship is to rely more and more on the grace of the Holy Spirit. This is the path to Christian maturity. This is how we "grow in Christ." There is a stage in our pilgrimage where this becomes particularly clear to us—a point in our discipleship at which we become *acutely* aware of our need of grace. And with this awareness comes the realization that we cannot meet that need in a haphazard way. We need help.

This is also true if we have been actively involved over the years in Christian service to the world. We probably realized quite soon that we could not change the world overnight. But we may not have perceived until now that the only way we can be effective at all is to be ready for the particular tasks Christ assigns to us. The key word is *obedience*, and here too we need help.

Perhaps these reasons touch on why you have felt the need to join a covenant discipleship group. In a word, you have come to a point of maturity in your Christian discipleship.

How will joining a covenant discipleship group affect my relationships with Christian friends or relatives who do not wish to join?

If you are asking this question, you are probably concerned that joining a covenant discipleship group might make other people in the church perceive you as a "super-Christian" or as someone who is going to put others on their best behavior. You are quite right to be concerned, because spiritual elitism, the feeling that some of us have the "inside track" with God, is not a desirable quality. You need to be sure that a covenant discipleship group will not do this to you, or to other people's perceptions of you.

This assurance can quickly be given. In fact, covenant discipleship groups fit into a congregation quite naturally. A good analogy is the church choir, which has a special role to play in the life and work of the church. In order to help with worship on a Sunday morning, the choir members agree to give up one night a week to practice. They have a talent, but they must apply themselves to use it; and when they do use it, it is for the benefit of the whole congregation. So we do not mind when they proceed through the sanctuary, distinctively robed, to prominent seats. After all, if we had the time and the inclination, we could join them; for very seldom is anyone excluded from a church choir because of voice quality.

"That's all very well," you may reply. "But covenant discipleship involves more than music and worship. In a covenant discipleship group I am going to be accountable for what I do in *all* the dimensions of my Christian discipleship—my good works, my spiritual disciplines, my very understanding of God's will in my life. Surely that is going to single me out in the congregation as someone whose lifestyle makes other people feel uncomfortable. I certainly don't want that to happen."

Don't worry, it won't. Or if it does, it will be the sort of give and take that happens all the time in congregational life. People will look on you and your covenant discipleship group as giving your time and energies to a disciplined walk with Christ, so that the whole congregation might have a better understanding of their own Christian commitment. They will begin to look to you for guidance and advice. You will become leaders in discipleship.

Moreover, because you are holding yourself accountable week by week, you will know better than anyone that you have no room whatsoever to brag.

What can I expect to happen in a covenant discipleship group?

The short answer is that you can expect to become more consistent, more reliable—in a word, more seasoned—in your Christian discipleship. But you probably want more of an answer than that.

To be more specific, therefore, you can expect three things to happen:

1. *You will become more aware of God's grace in your life.*

We should remember first of all that grace, God's constant initiative toward us, is extended with impeccable good manners. God will not force grace into our lives. We must *allow* it to work in and through us, and we are always given the right to refuse. Indeed, a good definition of human sin is the chronic tendency to resist God's gracious initiatives. As Christians, however, we have made a commitment to be open to grace. This means we accept responsibility for allowing God to work in our lives, and for obeying God's directives in our discipleship.

In the General Rule of Discipleship, there are four areas, based on the teachings of Jesus, in which we can actively allow grace to guide and shape our Christian discipleship. Two of these areas are the time-honored disciplines, or ordinances, of the church: acts of worship (the ministries of word and sacrament) and acts of devotion (prayer, searching the scriptures, and fasting or temperance). Knowing about these "means of grace" is one thing, but actually using or practicing them is another. The early Methodists knew this pitfall well, and they formed weekly class meetings to safeguard against it. Covenant discipleship groups are following their example, meeting together once a week so that the members can tell each other whether or not they have practiced these disciplines. You will find that this simple exercise in mutual accountability really works. The method was sound in Wesley's day, and it is just as effective today. If you know that you have to give an account to someone each week for something you know you should be doing, there is a much better chance that you will do it.

Thus, you can expect to become much more regular in your attendance at worship and sacrament, in your prayer life, and in your Bible study. Perhaps for the first time, you will begin the spiritual disciplines of fasting or temperance, and in the weekly covenant discipleship meetings you will engage in an intentional form of Christian communion, or fellowship.

These means of grace will give you new strength and vigor for your Christian life. This will not happen immediately, nor should it—any more than you should take 365 daily vitamins all at once to give you a year's worth of health. Nor will it happen predictably. Your times of richest blessing will catch you by surprise, and you will continue to have many times of routine worship and empty devotions. But most assuredly, as you open yourself consistently to grace, grace will empower your discipleship. From time to time, God will let you know that you are becoming one of the "seasoned" members of your church, as people begin to turn to you for guidance and advice about the deeper things of the faith. You acquire these insights only by disciplined practice.

2. You will find new ways of serving God and your neighbor in the world.

For many group members, this proves to be the most exciting dimension of covenant discipleship. When you begin your weekly meetings, you will probably find yourself where most of us are—bearing no one any ill will, and helping people in ways that make for good neighborly relations. Indeed, as a Christian, you have probably been quite intentional in this.

In your covenant discipleship group, however, you will discover opportunities for Christian service which you have never considered before. At first you may find this somewhat disconcerting, especially when you realize just how much wider the horizons of your neighborliness need to be stretched. But week by week, you will find yourself impelled by grace to serve newfound neighbors. Perhaps you will find them in prisons, among the homeless of the inner city, or among disadvantaged children struggling to survive the drug culture.

You will also be stimulated to a bolder and clearer vision of the kingdom of God, the new age of Jesus Christ; and you will acquire new insights into the need for the exercise of God's justice in the world. Perhaps you will be prompted to take a stand on issues such as the death penalty, political torture, racism, or world hunger. Perhaps you will find yourself having to stand against less dramatic injustices at your place of work—or even in your church. These involvements will be all the more unnerving if they are new for you. But always you will find God's grace sufficient for the tasks that Jesus assigns.

By the same token, even if you have long been involved in such activities, to be held accountable week by week for the whole of the new General Rule may bring new perspectives to your acts of compassion and acts of justice. As you stimulate others to reach out to those in need, in turn you will be touched by the need for small kindnesses close to home. Perhaps most important, you will find yourself drawing more consistently on grace for your vision and your power, and thus find your service in the world more truly obedient to Jesus Christ—a check on your discipleship which cannot be made too often.

3. You will find your understanding of God's will in your life greatly enhanced.

When Jesus instructed the first disciples to meet together in his name, with the promise that he would always be in their midst when they did so, he was not offering them a spiritual bonus. He was stating an axiom, indeed *the* axiom, of Christian discipleship: We need one another in order to discern the will of God.

The reasoning is quite straightforward. When you and I converse with God, one end of the line (so to speak) consists of a very imperfect receiver. Whatever God is trying to say to you or me, our own agendas are likely to get in the way. But when several of us gather together, each endeavoring to help the other to be Christian disciples, the pooling of insights is going to give each of us a better idea of what God is trying to do with our lives.

As you give an account of how you have tried to walk with Christ, you will help everyone else in the group with their discipleship, and they will help you with yours. Together you will arrive at a level of responsiveness to grace which none of you would have acquired on your own. Indeed, there is no better summary of the nature and purpose of a covenant discipleship group than this: It opens us to God's grace.

Chapter 7

Writing the Covenant

When the group has been formed, and the members have agreed on a day and time, the first task is to draw up the covenant that will be the basis for the weekly meetings. This should be a covenant of intent, consisting of a number of clauses which express the resolve of the members to carry out certain agreed disciplines and tasks. But it should also be a covenant of grace, with introductory and closing statements that ground it firmly in the work of the Holy Spirit.

THE NATURE OF COVENANT WITH GOD

The scriptural meaning of covenant is to enter willingly into a binding agreement with God. It is a response to God's gracious initiative which cannot later be undone, however difficult it might be to keep. It can only be broken.

Many scholars believe that the Hebrew word for covenant, *berith*, came from an Assyrian word, meaning a *shackle* or a *fetter*. This is because the people of God in Old Testament times learned the hard way that there is no greater captivity than to be enslaved to self-interest and self-gratification. The only true freedom is to be bound to God in faithful obedience (Exod. 19:4-5; Jer. 7:22-23). In the New Testament, this became the New Covenant of the Spirit, mediated through Jesus Christ, who himself fulfilled the law, and in whose service is perfect freedom (Acts 2:14-18; 2 Cor. 3:7-18; Gal. 5:16-18; Heb. 9:15).

The scripture makes clear, of course, that the people of Israel broke their covenant with God (Jer. 31:32; Heb. 8:9), just as the church time and again has broken the new covenant in Christ. It is a constant source of wonder that God is always faithful to these covenants even when the people of God are fickle and faithless

(Jer. 31:33-34; Ezek. 16:60-63; Hos. 2:14-23; Heb. 8:6-13). Yet such has been the pattern across centuries of Jewish and Christian history. This is why the supreme privilege of Christian discipleship is to be called into covenant, into this special relationship with the God of all creation. It is the only way we can even begin to live the sort of life God intends for us, and to avoid the slavery of self-interest and self-determination.

Thus the covenant of a covenant discipleship group is not an end in itself, and most certainly not a set of rules and regulations. Rather it is a dynamic means of grace, an instrument to help Christian disciples follow the leadings of God's Spirit in the world.

The sample on the following page illustrates the three components of a covenant of discipleship: the preamble, the clauses, and the conclusion.

THE PREAMBLE

The purpose of the preamble is to make clear that the clauses of the covenant are not a set of rigid regulations, but a shaping of Christian discipleship in response to God's grace. Thus, even though the covenant expresses strong intent, the preamble declares that the members are not going to be "graded" week by week.

The group may wish to adopt the preamble from the sample covenant, but they should feel free to change the wording, or to substitute something altogether different. The examples later in the chapter give some very good alternatives and show that the writing of the preamble often raises important points of faith and practice for the members.

Do not be concerned if this process takes several weeks. Allow each member to express his or her opinion as freely as possible. *Do* get concerned, however, if it seems that hairs are being split, or that the group is procrastinating. One of the most devious snares for a Christian is to talk about discipleship rather than to practice it!

THE CLAUSES

The most important thing to be said about the clauses is that each group writes its own covenant. There should be nothing in a covenant of discipleship on which every member of the group is

A SAMPLE COVENANT OF DISCIPLESHIP

Knowing that Jesus Christ died that I might have eternal life, I herewith pledge myself to be his disciple, witnessing to his saving grace, and seeking to follow his teachings under the guidance of the Holy Spirit. I faithfully pledge my time, my skills, my resources, and my strength, to search out God's will for me, and to obey.

I will worship each Sunday unless prevented.

I will receive the sacrament of Holy Communion each week.

I will pray each day, privately, and with my family or with friends.

I will read and study the scriptures each day.

I will return to Christ the first tenth of all I receive.

I will spend four hours each month to further the cause of the disadvantaged in my community.

When I am aware of injustice to others, I will not remain silent.

I will obey the promptings of the Holy Spirit to serve God and my neighbor.

I will heed the warnings of the Holy Spirit not to sin against God and my neighbor.

I will prayerfully care for my body and for the world in which I live.

I hereby make my commitment, trusting in the grace of God to give me the will and the strength to keep this covenant.

Date:_____ Signed:_____

not agreed, and which every member is not ready to adopt as a guiding principle of their discipleship. (The only exceptions to this are "personal clauses." See below, page 121.)

As with the preamble, there are often lengthy discussions before the content of a covenant is agreed. The group might want to use the sample covenant once again as a starting point—though it is most unlikely that these clauses will have everyone's agreement. For example, some may object to praying with friends as a daily exercise, or to allocating a fixed amount of time to the disadvantaged.

The group should therefore take as long as necessary in writing their clauses. These statements of intent will be the touchstone of their accountability, and the finished product should be a document that each member can wholeheartedly affirm in faith and practice.

THE GENERAL RULE OF DISCIPLESHIP

Having said all of this, there are nonetheless some guidelines for shaping the covenant, and we find these in the General Rule of Discipleship:

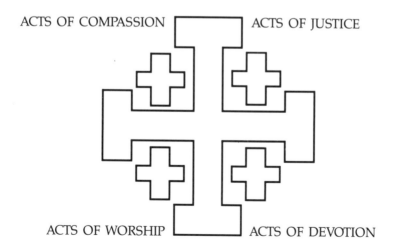

ACTS OF COMPASSION   ACTS OF JUSTICE

ACTS OF WORSHIP   ACTS OF DEVOTION

The importance of the General Rule in shaping the covenant is that it keeps these four dimensions of Christian discipleship in proper balance. There is no priority as to sequence. Acts of worship may begin the covenant, as in the sample on page 135; or they may conclude it. But no covenant should emphasize any one of these areas to the detriment of the others. They are all vital to an authentic Christian discipleship, and they are all a means of God's grace.

SPIRITUAL PROMPTINGS AND WARNINGS

There should also be clauses in the covenant to keep the group accountable for heeding and obeying the promptings and warnings of the Holy Spirit—the "nudges" we receive from God to do or say particular things at particular times, or to refrain from particular words and deeds.

We noted in chapter five the danger of self-deception when we rely solely on these spiritual directives for our discipleship—and thus our need of the guidelines in the General Rule. But "methodical" discipleship does not shut out the spontaneous work of the Holy Spirit in our lives. Quite the contrary, it enhances our discernment, so that we are more ready for spiritual promptings and warnings when they come.

This is an area in which many group members experience great difficulty. They are wary of using spiritual language to describe what they have always regarded as bright ideas, or hunches, or twinges of conscience. Yet learning to accept that these are promptings or warnings from God is precisely what makes this part of the covenant so exciting. The ordinary things of life take on new meaning as we come to understand that everything, even the mundane, is a spiritual work of grace.

LIVING IN THE WORLD

The principle underlying the clauses of a covenant is that they should all be practicable, both to attempt and to sustain. They should acknowledge that God's grace reaches people right where they are in the world, and that men and women can respond to this grace within the routines of daily living.

This follows the principle of discipleship we examined in the early Methodist class meeting: The Christian does not have to withdraw from the world, permanently or temporarily, in order to be in communion with God. The discipline of discipleship comes in learning how not to resist the gracious initiatives of the Holy Spirit in the immediacy of the world.

RESPONSIVENESS TO CONTEXT

In patterning a covenant discipleship group after these early Methodist classes, therefore, the clauses should reflect the worldly context of the group. Members should feel free to introduce clauses for a limited time in order to respond to particular situations, or to drop clauses that no longer require accountability. Likewise, groups will need to reconsider their covenants when they gain members. In this way, those who are new to a group can have ownership of the clauses also.

PRACTICALITY

A further word needs to be said about the practicality of the covenant. Without losing accountability for their discipleship, the group should refrain from introducing clauses at the outset of their covenant which any of the members find to be too demanding. The question always to be asked is whether a clause is "do-able"— whether it is something which everyone feels can be attempted.

This may mean initially reducing the requirements of a particular clause. Take, for example, the clause in the sample covenant concerning the eucharist: "I will receive the sacrament of Holy Communion each week." If there are group members who object to this, the wording may be changed to "each month"; and if there are still objections, to "regularly." Since it is an instituted means of grace, however, the clause should not be dropped altogether.

As another example, some members may object to the clause that states: "I will help at least one person in need each day." In this case, the wording may be changed to: "I will be sensitive to people in need, and help them when I can." Though again, as one of Jesus' directives, and as a component of the General Rule, the clause should not be dropped altogether.

"TAKING UP THE SLACK"

By the same token, as the covenant helps the group develop its discipleship, members will find that the discipline of weekly accountability begins to bite. This can happen in several ways. The group may discover that a clause which has hitherto received token attention during the weekly meetings suddenly acquires new meaning. A good case in point is the clause from the sample covenant which states: "I will heed the warnings of the Holy Spirit not to sin against God and my neighbor." After weeks of routine answers, someone may ask: "Who is my neighbor?" The answer Jesus gave to that question should immediately cause a stir.

Someone else may ask, "What is a warning of the Holy Spirit?" Once again, the group is likely to find itself involved in critical consciousness raising, as the meaning of divine guidance and inward discernment is revealed with new depth and power.

Perhaps the group has dealt with the clause on prayer in a somewhat perfunctory manner for quite some time. Then one of the members reports that her child asked her two days ago why they no longer say grace at mealtimes. Out of this comes a general confession from the group that no one is holding family prayers, and that something should be done about it.

At all such moments of growth—for growth it most certainly is— the group should consider "taking up the slack" by tightening the relevant clauses of their covenant. If prayer is a weakness, then an additional clause can be added to remedy the deficiency. If the warnings of the Holy Spirit not to sin against God and neighbor have not been heeded, or if the people who qualify as neighbor have not been recognized, then clauses should be made more specific. When people in need do not present themselves for help, perhaps group members should look for them; they are still out there in the world. When prayer or Bible reading tends to be neglected, appointments should be made—and *kept*.

In other words, the clauses of the covenant are not fixed; they are not inflexible. They are rather a resilient framework for a discipleship that will always be responsive to the grace of God. As with all healthy guidelines, they are designed, not to limit the scope of the Christian lifestyle, but to keep it in balance; not to legislate the works of grace in Christian discipleship, but to shape them. The acts of devotion, worship, compassion, and justice, exemplified by our forebears and taught by Jesus of Nazareth, are not ends in themselves. They are the means to an end, and that end is the worship and service of God in the world.

LENGTH OF THE COVENANT

There is no fixed number of clauses in a covenant. But the group should remember that the goal of the weekly meeting is to go through each clause with each member in one hour. In practice, therefore, a covenant should probably have no more than ten clauses—though if members wish to add more, there is no objection.

By the same token, clauses do not have to be in multiples of four in order to give each area of the General Rule equal emphasis. There are times in the life of the group when particular clauses will require very little attention during the group process, quite simply because everyone is doing them very well. But then the nature of the members' pilgrimages will change, and these same clauses will cause great difficulty, especially when they have begun to "bite."

The group should feel free to give more time to these "biting" clauses whenever they sense the need. Only when certain areas of the General Rule are being permanently neglected should the issue of balance be addressed.

KEEPING OUR BEARINGS

Maintaining this balance is rather like flying an aircraft. Once the plane is in the air at flying speed, it is very much a free agent. The pilot has to respond to the pressures of the air from all directions—up, down, and sideways. If the airflow is moving the plane too much to the right, then the pilot must fly it more to the left. But if the airflow changes, the control setting must be adjusted, or the plane will fly off course in another direction.

So it is with the Christian life. We are buffeted from every side (2 Cor. 4:8), and we have to respond in order to keep on course. Then we have to correct our response when the pressures change. This is why it is so important to keep our bearings (the General Rule) and to have a clear compass heading (Jesus Christ).

The weekly covenant discipleship meeting is a mutual checkpoint with trusted colleagues who are on the same journey.

PERSONAL CLAUSES

While each clause of the covenant must have the agreement of all members—something which, as we noted, usually means modifying certain clauses—some members may have special needs that cannot be met in this way. Someone may wish to be held accountable for a particular dimension of his or her discipleship that clearly does not concern anyone else in the group, yet which is of vital importance to the person concerned.

The group should respond to such requests by leaving some time at the conclusion of the meeting to hold the members accountable. These "personal clauses" do not have to be written down, but can be shared with the rest of the group week by week—especially since, by their very nature, they will tend to be of immediate and temporary importance.

THE CONCLUSION

When the writing of the clauses is completed, a short statement reaffirming the nature and purpose of the covenant should bring it to a conclusion. The wording in the sample covenant on page 115 can be used or adapted, though again, there are alternatives in the examples beginning on page 124.

By stressing that grace is the dynamic of our discipleship, the concluding declaration reminds the members of the group that they will not be striving to maintain standards or levels of performance. They will merely be applying the teachings of Jesus and trusting that the Holy Spirit will empower them for whatever tasks they are assigned in preparing for the reign of God.

SIGNING THE COVENANT

Once the covenant is agreed, someone in the group should accept responsibility for having it reproduced in a convenient format. The page size of this book is usually acceptable to everyone, making it suitable for folding into a wallet or purse for reference. Some groups have reduced their covenants to a small laminated card, making it even more convenient to carry around in a pocket. As in the sample on page 115, the covenant should have room for a signature and date. When copies have been distributed to each member, the first step at the next meeting should be to have each member sign her or his copy.

OPENENDED COMMITMENT

When the covenant is being signed, the members of the group need to understand that their commitment is openended. This is not an activity to be tried for a period and dropped if it is not immediately or always fulfilling. It is an agreement made with God and with the group to "watch over one another in love"; and if this agreement is not made willingly and unreservedly, the group will be burdened by doubts and pressures to succeed.

It is very important to make this clear at the outset. Of course the commitment is not to the same group. People will often move to different communities or places of work, and schedules will tend to change. Ours is a very mobile society. But as long as a member is able to attend covenant discipleship meetings, the other members need the assurance of that commitment. Unavoidable absences should be announced to the group in advance or excused as soon as possible afterwards. If a member is absent, and no one knows why, someone from the group should contact that person, not only to say how much he or she was missed, but also to ask for an explanation; the covenant, once accepted, is binding on everyone.

LEAVING THE GROUP

It should further be made clear when the covenant is signed that there is only one valid reason for leaving a group: the strong sense of vocation that one's discipleship can be better fulfilled in other ways. If a member reaches such a decision prayerfully, then departure from the group should be intentional. It should be communicated to the other members in one of the weekly meetings and implemented promptly. Experience shows, however, that when the nature of the commitment is made clear at the outset, very few people leave covenant discipleship groups.

RADICAL FREEDOM

All of this may seem to be very demanding, if not legalistic. Yet it is exactly how Jesus called his first disciples. He did not ask Simon, Andrew, James, or John if they would like to accompany him for a while—to see if they liked it, or if they found his teachings fulfilling. Jesus gave them radical freedom to answer him with a "yes" or with a "no." Along with the radical freedom, however, came radical responsibility. And this, as we have argued throughout this study, is precisely what we lack in our discipleship today.

There are those who argue that true freedom of choice requires a number of options—the "multiple choice" to which we were all conditioned at high school. Yet there is a serious flaw to this argument, which is rarely exposed for what it is. In order for "multiple choice" to be available, someone, somewhere, has to determine what those choices are. And as any student can testify, a "multiple choice" examination will usually reveal far more about the teacher than the subject.

This is why the invitation of Jesus is so radically free. God does not attempt to mislead us by claiming to offer us options which, with all their multiplicity, are in point of fact highly restrictive. Instead we are offered the freedom to go our own way with all the enslavement of self-centeredness and self-fulfillment, or to go the way of Jesus of Nazareth with all the freedom of being his disciples.

SOME COVENANT PREAMBLES

The following preambles are a small selection from the many covenants which covenant discipleship groups have sent to the Nashville office over the years. While each covenant has been distinctive, there has also been a clear and encouraging trend: Some of the most imaginative and original writing has come from college and seminary campuses.

From a covenant discipleship group at Lake Ronkomkoma UMC, New York

Having been called by Jesus Christ to be disciples, with awe and trembling hearts, we answer his call to be Doorkeepers. This group shall exist for the purpose of support, communal prayer, receiving the Word, and watching over one another in love so that all are encouraged to work out their salvation and offer others Christ.

Christian disciples need a firm foundation of faith. Paul urges the church at Ephesus to "grow up in every way into Christ" so that they may no longer be children "tossed to and fro and carried about by every wind of doctrine" (Eph. 4:13-15). To that end, that we may grow toward maturity of faith and celebrate as a community God's presence with us and the gifts God has given us to use for the furthering of the kingdom, we expect of all who join us: . . .

From a covenant discipleship group at Wesley Theological Seminary, Washington, DC

In gratitude for the grace of Jesus Christ, in whose death we have died and in whose resurrection we have found new life, we pledge to be his disciples. We recognize that our time and talents are gifts from God, and we will use them to search out God's will for us and to obey it.

We will do our best not to compromise the will of God for human goals. We will serve both God and God's creation earnestly and lovingly. We respect and accept fully all group members, whose integrity and confidentiality we will uphold in all that we share. With God's grace and their help we covenant to: . . .

From a seminar held at the Nebraska Conference Fellowship of Learning

Called into being and empowered by the grace of God, we covenant to dedicate ourselves to a life that exemplifies Christ and the gospel. We offer our time, talents, abilities, and resources, in obedience to the gospel, acknowledging our dependence upon God's grace and the power of the Holy Spirit.

From the sample covenant for Branch Groups, Covenant Discipleship for Youth

Knowing that Jesus Christ died for me and that God calls me to be a disciple of Jesus Christ, I desire to practice the following disciplines in order that I might know God's love, forgiveness, guidance, and strength. I desire to make God's will my own and to be obedient to it. I desire to remain in Christ with the help of this covenant so that I might bear fruit for the kingdom of God.[44]

From a student covenant discipleship group at University UMC, College Park, MD

To be a Christian disciple means sharing in Christ's ongoing work of salvation in the world. The task of discipleship therefore calls for the binding together of those with like mind and purpose, to watch over one another in love.

- We covenant together to be present each week.
- We will open and close our meetings with prayer—to help us focus our minds and hearts on God rather than on ourselves and our accomplishments.
- We will approach each other with honesty and in a spirit of love. Understanding that our purpose is not to judge each other, we will hopefully feel free to speak honestly—both in terms of our keeping with the covenant as well as our failure to do so.
- As Christ does for us, so will we try, to the best of our ability, to "watch over each other in love."
- We covenant together to offer encouragement to each other to grow in faith.[45]

From a student covenant discipleship group on the campus of the University of Arizona, Tucson

"I love thee, O Lord, my strength. The Lord is my rock, and my fortress, and my deliverer, my God, my rock, in whom I take refuge, my shield, and the horn of my salvation, my stronghold. I call upon the Lord, who is worthy to be praised" (Ps. 18:1-3a RSV).

As Christians, we acknowledge God's unconditional love and acceptance of all [God's] creation. God is alive in us and guides us in our journey of faith. With these things in mind we will support and encourage each other in our efforts to follow God's plan for our lives. We will strive to recognize God as: strength, salvation, love, peace, inspirer, comforter, friend, hope, joy.

In order to more fully develop our relationship with God we covenant to do the following: . . . [46]

SOME COVENANT CLAUSES

The following sample clauses are also taken from covenants sent to the Nashville office. Some of them are from the earliest groups, and some from the most recent, but all are clauses that groups have used at one time or another. This gives them a ring of authenticity, and a down-to-earth quality.

No Neat Categories

Several points about these clauses are worth noting. First of all, while they are arranged according to the General Rule of Discipleship, not all of them can strictly be defined as acts of worship, justice, devotion, or compassion. Indeed, in some instances there is considerable overlap and even duplication—as in the clauses dealing with various aspects of stewardship.

This illustrates an important principle of the General Rule, or of anything to do with Christian discipleship: We should not get caught up in method for its own sake. It is far more important to have covenant clauses which are meaningful and relevant to the Christian life than to have them neatly classified. Moreover, as we noted in the previous chapter, some spiritual disciplines today have become almost faddish and can only be incorporated into covenants with some care.

Progressive Accountability

Another point worth noting is that a number of clauses have been selected in order to illustrate the ways in which groups deepen the insight and conviction of their accountability by making their clauses more specific, or more "biting." Sometimes this is reflected in the frequency with which they intend to put the clause into practice; sometimes it is indicated by the directness with which the clause names particular disciplines or tasks.

Whenever groups change the clauses of their covenants, almost always they make them more demanding. This is not an expression of over-achievement, but merely an indication that grace is at work in their lives, and that they are beginning to chew on the "meat" of the gospel.

Christ the Only Paradigm

One final word about these clauses is that they are included solely as examples, in the hope that they can assist groups in the writing of their covenants. They are certainly not meant as a paradigm for discipleship, since each group must forge its own clauses and must agree on its own covenant. Christ, and Christ alone, is the paradigm for our discipleship. In this way, the Holy Spirit will have unique guidance for each group.

ACTS OF COMPASSION

I* will do all I can to help people in need.

I will seek out people in need and
do all I can to help them.

We* will strive to increase our service to others and
graciously acknowledge others' service to us.

I will go two miles for a sister or a brother
who asks me to go one.

I will spend one hour each week visiting a lonely ✓
person whom I would not ordinarily visit.

I will spend at least one hour each day
helping someone in need.

I will spend four hours each month helping
the disadvantaged in my community.

I will spend four hours each week helping
the disadvantaged in my community.

We will balance the time we devote to school, church,
work, family, and friends, including
our own spiritual and recreational life.

I will spend an hour each day with my children. ✓

I will spend some time each day with each member of
my family in meaningful communication.

We will practice listening to other people
as a ministry of grace.

*The use of the personal "I" or the collective "We" is entirely at the discretion of each group.

Music in Nursing Homes each month - ✓

I will express feelings of genuine appreciation to
at least one person each day.

We will engage in regular visits to local prisons.

I will make weekly visits to local prisons.

We will each establish a meaningful relationship with
someone in prison and, where possible, with their families.

I will get to know at least one poor family.

I will offer friendship each day to someone
of an ethnic background different from my own.

We will encourage our congregation in its missional
giving, and do this by personal example.

I will seek to help a family in need somewhere
else in the world.

I will eat one less meal each day
and give the money to feed the hungry.

ACTS OF DEVOTION

We will practice daily devotions, including the reading ✓
of scripture and prayer for group members.

I will pray each day, privately and publicly.

I will spend at least one hour each day in the
disciplines of praise, thanksgiving, confession,
petition, intercession, and meditation.

I will pray daily in solitude and with my family or
friends. I will include all the members of my
covenant discipleship group in my daily prayers.

I will keep a diary to plan my daily and weekly prayers.

We will make the study of scripture a central part
of our daily devotions.

We will agree on our daily Bible readings and share
our insights as we give an account each week.

I will record the spiritual insights of my
daily Bible reading.

I will read the Bible each day as a devotional
exercise, not as a study assignment.

We will each keep a spiritual journal and will   *weekly* ✓
devote time at the end of each day to enter our
reflections as the Holy Spirit leads us.

I will spend at least thirty minutes each day alone
with God, of which fifteen minutes will be spent
just listening to God.

I will pray each day for my enemies.

I will take the initiative each day in holding
family devotions.

I will read only those materials and watch only those programs which enhance my discipleship.

✓   I prayerfully pledge to practice responsible stewardship of my God-given resources: my body, the environment, my artistic graces, and my intellectual gifts.

In order to care for our individual wholeness in body, mind, and spirit, we will schedule time each week for retreat, reflection, renewal, and fun.

Knowing that my body is the temple of God, I will prayerfully plan my work and leisure time.

I will seek the guidance of the Holy Spirit in fasting.

ACTS OF JUSTICE

I will endeavor to oppose injustice, in whatever form.

When I am aware of injustices practiced in my church,
my community, my nation, and the world, I will speak out.

We will not be silent when confronted with social injustice,
and we will witness for justice, inclusiveness, and
equality, and will encourage reconciliation wherever possible.

I will stand up for those who are not present or able
to stand up for themselves.

I will actively support a movement for world peace.

I will communicate regularly with my elected
national representatives on issues of world peace.

I will get to know at least one unemployed person.

I will communicate regularly with my elected local
representatives on issues of unemployment and
economic justice.

I will get to know at least one person of a different
ethnic background at my place of work.

We will become more aware of social situations through
attention to the news (newspapers, television, magazines, radio).

I will ask forgiveness of God each day for those who die ✓
of starvation, and I will work to alleviate world hunger.

We will become an advocacy group for prisoners of
religious and political conscience.

As a group, we will speak out whenever God's justice ✓
is ignored by our leaders at work, (at church,)
in our nation, and in the world.

Once each month, lift up injustice at church —

We will devote our daily Bible study to the eighth century prophets for the whole of the coming year.

I will dissociate myself from racial slurs and jokes at my place of work.

I will express disapproval of racial, social, and sexual prejudice among my relatives and friends.

We will practice responsible stewardship of the world's resources in the context of our personal lives and communal commitments.

We will each take action to improve our relationship with our natural environment.

I will strive for unconditional love and acceptance of all God's creations.

✓ I will pray every day for the coming of the reign of God.

ACTS OF WORSHIP

I will be faithful in attendance and participation
in worship each Sunday.

On Vacation, etc. (

We will participate in weekly corporate worship,
striving for true involvement.

I will seek opportunities for worship at least once
each week in addition to Sunday.

I will receive the sacrament of Holy Communion each
week, when possible in my covenant discipleship group.

We will receive the sacrament of Holy Communion daily.

We will prayerfully consider what resources we can
contribute each week to the work of Christ in the world.

I will return to Christ the first tenth of ✓
all that I receive.

We will pray for those who lead us in worship each
week, and especially for the preacher.

We will pray for those who visit our worship service,
that they will be touched by grace.

We will pray for those who are baptized in our church
and visit the parents of baptized children.

SPIRITUAL PROMPTINGS AND WARNINGS

I will listen to the promptings of the Spirit as they
affect others' well-being.

I will be honest in all things at my place of work.

We will strive to express ourselves fruitfully to
those around us.

I will witness to my faith in Christ at least once each day.

I will remember that whatever I do—be it work, study, or
recreation—is dedicated to God.

We will seek out ways to yield our all to God's
saving grace.

I will be truthful in reporting to my covenant discipleship
group whenever I disobey a spiritual prompting,
or fail to heed a spiritual warning.

I will set aside a specific time for personal spiritual
renewal each week.

As a group we will spend a day in retreat twice each year.

We will be available to each other at all times for
support and prayer in times of spiritual testing.

✓   I will not let the sun set on my anger.

SOME COVENANT CONCLUSIONS

Knowing that the grace of God works in each of us,
I pray that my heart will be opened to God's presence, that
my eyes will be opened to see the sorrows and joys of God's
creatures, and that my ears will be opened to hear God's will
so that I will have the strength to keep this covenant
with each of the other members.
By affixing my signature to this document, the
singular "I" becomes the communal "We."

———————————

We therefore pledge our commitment to God and to
the group, that the choices we make in our daily
journeys will enhance our growth as Christians, honor
our creator and Redeemer, and minister to our world.

———————————

Recognizing that there are times when we cannot
live up to the standards we have set for ourselves, we
covenant to support each other in an encouraging and
constructive manner.

———————————

Trusting in grace, we pledge to support each other
as we leave the confines of comfort in our search to do
God's will in the world.

A COVENANT FROM PRISON

As a final example, the following covenant comes from a covenant discipleship group formed in federal prison by Glenn Bradley, a member of St. James United Methodist Church in Little Rock, Arkansas. The story of how Glenn came to serve time, and how his covenant discipleship groups at St. James and in prison helped him to a deeper walk with Christ, appeared in the April/July 1990 issue of the *Covenant Discipleship Quarterly*.

Knowing that Jesus Christ died that I might have eternal
life, I hereby make my commitment to be Christ's disciple,
holding nothing from him, but yielding all to the
gracious initiatives of the Holy Spirit.

1. I will search out God's will for me and obey, not compromising God's will for human goals.

2. I will spend time alone with God each day (including prayer and scripture) and I will lift up to the Lord each member of our covenant discipleship group.

3. I will not hesitate to acknowledge God's presence in my life and to share the Good News of Jesus Christ when prompted by the Holy Spirit.

4. I will be slow to take offense and will prayerfully seek each day to forgive others and myself.

5. I will refrain from cursing, talking bad of others, name calling, excessive anger, and fighting. Also, I will be just in all of my dealings.

6. I will worship each Sunday unless prevented.

7. I will faithfully care for my body as the temple of the Lord.

8. I will be sensitive to those in need and live out my faith in good works to my fellow man, utilizing the gifts which God gave each of us: time, talents, and material resources.

9. I will fast one day each week.

10. I will share in Christian fellowship each week, where I will be accountable for my discipleship.

I hereby make my commitment, trusting in the Holy Spirit and grace of Jesus Christ to work in me that I might have the strength to keep my covenant.

SOME COMMON QUESTIONS

Because the covenant is so central to the life and work of covenant discipleship groups, many questions are asked about its nature and purpose. The following are the ones most frequently raised, along with some answers.

Why do we need a covenant?

We need a covenant in a covenant discipleship group because a covenant relationship with God is the foundation of Christian discipleship. We make our covenant in response to the gracious initiative of the Holy Spirit. God promises to accept us as family, with all of the privileges that family brings. Our part is to accept our new family obligations, joyfully serving God in every way we can.

But if our covenant is with God, why do we need to make a covenant with each other?

This question is more difficult to answer today than once it might have been. In our generation, contracts tend to be taken seriously only when they prove convenient, and this attitude has infected the church. Most covenants made by Christians today, whether with God or with one another, are of very short duration. We plan their obsolescence, preparing at the outset for the time when we might not want to keep them any more. In short, the word *covenant* has become seriously devalued; and not incidentally, a great deal of discipleship has become a loose option.

If we take our discipleship seriously, however, and regard the keeping of our word as a point of honor, then a covenant with each other makes very good sense. For of two things we can be sure in our covenant relationship with God: (1) God will always be faithful; (2) many times we will not. Accordingly, those of us who are concerned about being good disciples should at least seek to minimize our faithlessness, and do all we can to avoid breaking our covenant with God.

This is what makes the covenant with each other so important. As with most things in life, the best way to ensure that we do something faithfully is to do it with others of like mind and purpose. A covenant with other Christians provides us with the mutual support and accountability we need in order to keep our covenant with God.

Does the covenant tend to become legalistic?

Not when we remember that we enter into it mutually and willingly. Moreover, the wording of the covenant contains nothing that does not have the consensus of the group.

Does a written covenant inhibit the freedom of grace?

Not at all. On the contrary, without an agreed statement of intent such as the covenant, it is all too easy for Christians to shape their discipleship around their own perceptions of God's will. This has rightly been labeled "cheap grace"—a grace always readily adaptable to personal preferences and even prejudices.

The freedom of grace in Christian discipleship is not the freedom to live our lives as we wish, but to avoid the enslavement of our own desires and ambitions. Indeed, the most important discovery of Christian discipleship is to realize how ill-equipped we are to run our own lives. The covenant of discipleship helps us to hold fast to the freedom of God's will rather than our own—to surrender an illusory freedom for the true freedom of binding ourselves to Christ.

But why does this have to take the form of a written covenant?

Because there are certain basic guidelines for discipleship which Christians across the centuries have found to be trustworthy. Wesley summarized these as works of mercy and works of piety, which today we have incorporated into the General Rule of Discipleship as acts of compassion, acts of devotion, acts of justice, and acts of worship.

However much we advance in the Christian life, we never outgrow the need for these basics. The Holy Spirit will increasingly empower us in our discipleship, but the *form*ality of a written covenant provides the *form* of how we live it out in the world, a framework within which we deepen our relationship with Christ while holding fast to the priorities of our service.

Once written, can the covenant be changed?

Indeed it can. In fact, it *ought* to be changed, regularly. Groups should routinely review the usefulness of particular clauses, and by consensus make changes as often as desirable or necessary.

What sorts of changes should be made?

Interestingly, a pattern has emerged over the years as groups have reported the changes in their covenants. Occasionally groups will relax clauses that have proved to be too demanding. But much more often, they will "tighten" their clauses rather than "loosen" them. In other words, as grace shapes their discipleship, members wish to be held *more* rather than *less* accountable.

When we remember that the Hebrew word for covenant probably came from the Assyrian for "shackle" or "fetter," and that the Jews were "bound" in covenant to God, we can see that the word still retains its power.

Chapter 8

The Group Meeting

ONLY ONE STRICT RULE

When the group has written and signed its covenant, it is ready to begin its regular weekly meetings. The one hard and fast rule for these sessions is that they should last only *one hour*. Meetings should begin punctually, whether or not everyone has arrived, and should end promptly, even if they began a little late. If the group wishes to remain longer, the meeting should still be officially ended. An informal time of sharing can then continue for as many as wish to stay.

Some groups feel that this is an unduly strict approach, and that spontaneous fellowship should not be so regulated. But that is exactly the point: Covenant discipleship groups are not designed for spontaneous fellowship, even though a great deal of it occurs. They are designed for mutual accountability, and in a very real sense they are business meetings—the business of Christian discipleship. Every member needs to know from the outset, therefore, that one hour is the only time that will be required of them. This way they are free to plan other activities, before or after the meeting.

ANY TIME, ANY DAY

This allows the group to schedule its sessions at any time of the day, on any day of the week; and that is what has happened over the years. Groups meet at 6:00 A.M. on Monday morning, 10:00 P.M. on Sunday night, and at many times in between. The noon hour is popular for those who can get away at lunchtime, and many members "brown bag" it. Some groups meet in the late afternoon, between leaving work and returning home. Others meet at 6:30 P.M. on Wednesday, just before most churches plan their midweek activities. And a very popular time is late afternoon or early evening on Sunday, for the same reason. Few groups meet on Sunday morning, however, since covenant discipleship is in no way designed to substitute for the Sunday school class.

Once a regular time has been agreed, and the groups are holding their weekly meetings, most members are very grateful for the firm limit of one hour. People who need to get to work after an early morning meeting, or back to work after a noon meeting, can count on a prompt conclusion, and this helps to regularize their commitment.

Indeed, a strong argument in favor of a covenant discipleship group is that it does not require a whole morning or afternoon or evening. It can readily be scheduled in conjunction with other activities. Besides this, the nature of the agenda is such that people do not have to make extensive preparations, administratively, intellectually, or emotionally. One only has to come prepared to be honest with one's Christian colleagues, and with God.

A REGULAR MEETING PLACE

Having selected a day and time, the group should then try to determine a regular meeting place. There is no problem about moving to a different place each week, but there is a drawback. People need to remember the different arrangements, and moving around can often leave them uncertain about where they are supposed to meet. To find somewhere relatively convenient for everyone is therefore the best solution. Exceptions can always be made if need be.

This is why, even though there is nothing against meeting in homes, offices, factories, or shops, most groups opt to meet in a room at their church—though some care should be taken in selecting the room. The agenda may be established by the covenant, and the format may be quite structured; but there is still a degree of intimacy in a covenant discipleship meeting, and the members need to feel free to express themselves in an atmosphere of confidentiality. Large rooms should be avoided, for example, as should places where interruptions are likely. The group should feel completely at ease during the whole of the hour.

If a regular meeting place is not possible, or if members prefer to take turns offering hospitality for the group, then it should be clearly stated at the conclusion of each meeting where the next one will take place. This information should also be given to any absent members as soon as possible. One of the worst things a group can do to itself is to have people guessing each week about where they are going to meet.

LEADING THE GROUP

Each session of the group needs to have a leader, selected at the conclusion of the previous meeting. This is not a permanent role, but one that rotates, with each member taking her or his turn at leading. The role is quite different from that of the early Methodist class leader, emphasizing that covenant discipleship groups are not a copy of the early class meeting, but an adaptation.

The rotation of the role of leader is explained on page 148, along with other dimensions of the group leadership. But one thing does need to be said at this stage: If any member is hesitant about accepting a turn, the point should not be pressed. Everyone should be encouraged to assume the responsibility in due course, and should be given every support when he/she does. But leading the meeting is not a condition of belonging to the group.

Thus it is often helpful to have a leader appointed for the first few weeks. If there is a member who has had some experience in group dynamics, that person is the logical choice; or if the pastor is a member of the group, he or she can assume the role. Once the form of the meetings has become familiar to all the members, however, the leadership should rotate.

CATECHESIS: QUESTION AND ANSWER

The most important reason for this sharing of leadership is that the format of the group meeting is what the early church called *catechesis*, a process of questions and answers. In other words, the distinctive dynamic of covenant discipleship is a dialogue between the leader and each member of the group. This was how the primitive Christian community taught its new members and its children: the *catechist* was the questioner, and the learners were called *catechumens*.[47] To this day in a number of denominations, learning one's *catechism* is still the first step toward being accepted into full church membership.

Of course, the content of the catechesis in covenant discipleship groups is practical rather than doctrinal. But the method is the same, and it is a good one. It means that important aspects of Christian discipleship are first of all agreed and written into the covenant. Then the leader appointed for the week voices them and asks each member to do likewise. In this way the axioms of living a Christian life are written, heard, and spoken.

To return for a moment to the illustration of flying an aircraft, this is precisely what is done in a cockpit prior to takeoff. There is a basic checklist—so basic that most pilots know it backwards. Yet the routine is established. However well they know these basics, the pilots go through them, one by one. They read them out to each other, they physically check that each control is properly set, and they say out loud that they have made the check. The procedure is rudimentary yet very necessary, for human error is always a real possibility.

How much more, then, should Christians do the same for their discipleship. After all, serving Jesus Christ in the world is the most responsible duty assigned to human beings in this world. It surely merits meticulous checking, for human error is an ever-present possibility.

OPENING THE MEETING

The group meetings should always be opened with prayer, either by the leader for the week, or by another member. The prayer should be quite short, being primarily a request for the guidance of the Holy Spirit throughout the hour, and for an openness on the part of the members to whatever God's grace might seek to accomplish. It is important that everyone be ready, not only for assurance and sympathetic understanding from the other members, but also for firmness and even correction. This attitude of readiness can be accomplished at the outset with a rightly worded prayer.

READING THE COVENANT

Many groups then find it helpful to have the entire covenant read out, either by the leader or by the group as a whole.

Some members find this to be a little reminiscent of elementary school, and resent the implications. Yet it should be remembered that the wording of the covenant has been laboriously honed. In many instances the result is a very eloquent document, as the samples in the preceding chapter illustrate. Far more often than not, the covenant merits an oral reading. After all, it is the bedrock of the group.

THE COVENANT CLAUSES

After the opening prayer and the reading of the covenant, each clause of the covenant is then taken in turn as a point of accountability. Beginning with herself or himself, the leader asks each member whether the intent expressed in the clause has been fulfilled during the past week. Only when each member has answered does the leader proceed to the next clause.

The questions are asked without any implied judgment, but rather as a means of sharing a joint pilgrimage, and of "watching over one another in love." If the clause was fulfilled, were there any noteworthy happenings or experiences that might help other group members in their journey? If the clause has not been fulfilled, were any special difficulties encountered? Can the group be of any help to the member in observing the clause more faithfully?

The accompanying diagram shows how this dynamic differs from other types of group discussion, and how important the role of the leader is in maintaining its flow. This is why it is helpful to have the leadership assigned for the first few weeks to a member who has some appreciation of group dynamics. But it is also why it is important to have it rotate as soon as possible.

The diagram illustrates the point very clearly. If the role of leader is permanently assigned to one person, then that person does not really have the opportunity to share in the process of mutual accountability. For one thing, the leader must always keep an eye on the time, making sure that things flow toward the end of the hour, and not past it. The leader must also make it possible for all members to participate, encouraging contributions from some, but keeping overly talkative members in check.

In other words, leading the group is hard work. And if that workload is not shared among all of the members, one member of the group (i.e., the leader) is going to be at a permanent disadvantage.

FIGURE 1. Flow of conversation in a covenant discipleship group

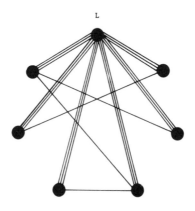

The process of question and answer gives the
leader a directive role.

FIGURE 2. Flow of conversation in a typical small group

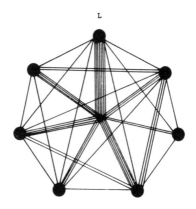

All of the members may interact, with the leader
playing a non-directive role.

COVERING ALL THE CLAUSES

As far as possible, the entire covenant should be covered each week. However, as groups develop their relationships, and as people begin to talk about their discipleship more openly, it may not be possible to go through all of the clauses in the time available. The leader should therefore exercise discretion as to which clauses will be covered during the meeting, and the group should be ready to be accountable the following week for any clauses that have had to be omitted.

The leader may also combine several clauses into one round of catechesis. For example, prayer and Bible study may be taken together; particular clauses concerning acts of compassion may be combined, as may clauses concerning acts of justice; worship and sacrament can readily be taken together; and temperance or fasting may be linked with clauses on spiritual promptings.

Combining clauses is often necessary during the early meetings of the group. As we have noted, it is a good idea to allocate part of the hour during the first few months to reflecting on the discussion questions following Chapters One through Five. If the group does this, there will certainly not be time to go through all the clauses. By the same token, if members are having some difficulty with a particular clause, they may wish to spend some time discussing or revising it, likewise limiting the time for answering the other clauses.

The guideline to be followed here is that no aspect of the covenant should be *regularly* postponed or combined. If this starts to happen, then the group should reconsider its covenant and perhaps make some revisions. For if there are clauses which are not a vital part of the group's accountability, they will work to the detriment of the covenant as a whole. The group should deal promptly with such issues and not avoid them.

CONTROLLED DIALOGUE

The leader should always keep in mind that the purpose of the group is to be accountable to the covenant. This should not make the conduct of the meeting unduly rigid, but neither should the conversation be allowed to digress into matters of general or casual interest. This is where the format of *catechesis*, or question and answer, proves to be helpful in keeping the meeting on course. The occasional exchange between other members should certainly be allowed as a spontaneous dimension of the meeting, but the leader should resume the role of *catechist* as soon as possible.

The skill to be acquired in this *catechesis* is primarily that of controlled dialogue—known in small group terminology as "feedback." At times, a group member will need to be encouraged to reply to a clause with more than a yes or no. Another member may need to be discouraged from dominating the conversation with lengthy accounts of personal experiences.

"ADVISE, REPROVE, COMFORT OR EXHORT"

The extent to which the meeting is handled tactfully but firmly will depend largely on the feedback given by the leader in response to each of the members. It is the leader who must move through the covenant at an appropriate pace and determine whether an extended exchange with a member can be of value to everyone else. It is likewise the leader who, as Wesley put it, must "advise, reprove, comfort or exhort" the members, offering guidance, correction, affirmation, or encouragement.

These skills are not acquired right away, but they come much more readily than in many small groups, in part because of the rotation of leadership, but also because of the commitment of the group to a *mutual* accountability. The more each person practices leadership skills when it is his or her turn, the more honest the group becomes in its accountability, and the more effective the members become in their discipleship.

POLITE RATHER THAN INTENSE

There will be times when the group experiences deep Christian communion. This is bound to increase as the group members develop their relationships, and it is to be welcomed. It should not, however, become the objective of the meeting. The leader should ensure that the purpose of each session remains accountability for the covenant. More intimate communion may well be a spiritual bonus, but it should not be an expectation which burdens the group. A meeting which is formal, or even mechanical, is just as important for the integrity of the group as one that is rich in spiritual sharing—indeed, in the long run, probably more important.

In a word, the tone of the weekly meetings is polite rather than intense. Although this may be an initial disappointment to some members who are searching for meaningful experiences of community, it is ultimately a source of profound reassurance. For it means that covenant discipleship groups do not get out of their depth—one of the persistent pitfalls of small groups, especially in congregational settings.

In the past forty years, numerous studies have demonstrated that people behave differently in small groups and tend to be more vulnerable to their feelings. In the hands of a skilled professional, this vulnerability can be used to great therapeutic effect, and often is. But in the hands of unskilled amateurs, or worse, left to their own devices, people in small groups will often say things they did not mean to say, and react in ways they subsequently find embarrassing or even humiliating.

The catechesis of covenant discipleship, and the agenda of an agreed covenant of intent, are important safeguards against such a pitfall. The weekly meetings are much more concerned with what people have *done* than with what they feel, and this prevents delving into areas group members are not equipped to handle. It also means that they can function very effectively without professional leadership.

PERSONAL PROBLEMS

Even so, personal problems will emerge from time to time during the group meetings, and members should certainly not feel inhibited about raising them. Nor should other members in the group regard them as an intrusion. They may give the group an opportunity to help the member concerned, and it may prove helpful to others who have the same problem.

Once again, however, the leader should not allow personal problems to distract the group from the covenant. A helpful solution can be to introduce the next clause, but at the same time offer to stay behind at the end of the meeting to talk further, asking other group members who can stay afterwards to do the same. This allows the person who raised the problem to consider how much he or she really wants to talk about it. It also provides an opportunity to assess whether it is something that really ought to be referred to the pastor.

CLOSING THE MEETING

As with the opening, so meetings should be closed with prayer. This can take a number of forms, from a brief benediction to a time of intercession. Individual concerns can also be shared with the group and then presented to God with full agreement.

Some groups find it meaningful to ask the pastor of the church to join them for the closing minutes, to celebrate a brief service of Holy Communion. This is particularly meaningful where several groups are meeting at the same time and in the same location. Having gone through their respective covenants, they can come together in one room for this closing act of worship. Where the pastor or other ordained clergy are members, groups are able to close with communion whenever they wish. But for groups without a clergy member, few pastors would not be very willing to celebrate the eucharist in this way. Of all the duties of the ordained ministry, that is surely the highest privilege.

HOUSEKEEPING

Various other items of housekeeping should be attended to before the meeting is finally closed. First, if there are any personal clauses for which individual members have asked the group to hold them accountable, these should be covered (see above, p. 121). Likewise, if there are personal clauses for the next week, they should be noted.

Then it should be agreed who will be the leader for next week. Once the group is well established in its routines, serving as leader does not require any major preparation. But during the first few months, and especially for those who have not done this sort of thing before, it is helpful to have a week's notice. And it is always a good thing for the leader to be able to prepare for the meeting prayerfully.

Another housekeeping item is that members of the group should share responsibility for contacting anyone who was not present.

Usually the absence is due to unforeseen circumstances. But it is always good to be held accountable, and thus to maintain the integrity of the covenant. Besides this, if the absent member proves to need help in some way, the group can quickly respond or notify the pastor.

Last, the group should always be clear about any particular aspects of their discipleship on which they need to act: in compassion, justice, worship, and devotion; or in obeying the promptings and warnings of the Holy Spirit. A final declaration of intent at the end of the weekly meeting can make all the difference.

CONVENERS

These housekeeping matters have resulted in the emergence of another leadership role in covenant discipleship groups: *conveners*. Unlike the group leadership, which rotates each week, the position of convener is a continuous appointment, and is filled when the covenant discipleship group is first formed, usually following a covenant discipleship weekend.

As the name indicates, conveners are the persons through whom the pastor or the church office can reach everyone in the groups. In turn, they keep the pastor notified about the progress of their groups, or any problems they might be having. The responsibilities are not heavy, but they are vital; and in congregations with a number of covenant discipleship groups, regular meetings of the conveners with the pastor become very important indeed. Quite apart from administrative details, such as keeping up to date with membership and days and times of meetings, there is the need for deeper resourcing as the groups grow in their discipleship. These and other questions concerning the life and health of covenant discipleship groups are dealt with in the companion volume, *Forming Christian Disciples* (order no. DR093).

As with anything in the life and work of the church, if covenant discipleship groups are neglected, or taken for granted, they will not thrive. And since covenant discipleship is a long-term commitment, all the more do the groups require careful and constant oversight. If your group does not have a convener, you should appoint one as soon as possible.

A SAMPLE GROUP MEETING

Perhaps the best way to illustrate all of this is to present a role play of an actual group meeting. As with all such "textbook" examples, the conversation is stereotyped and even stilted. But the dialogue is drawn from recollections of actual group meetings, and from reports we have received over the years in the covenant discipleship office. To that extent, therefore, it has some authenticity.

It is not necessary to present the whole of a covenant discipleship meeting. What follows includes the opening and closing procedures, and a number of representative clauses. There are six members in this group, including the leader. Rather than risk giving them fictitious names, they are merely described as "First Member," "Second Member," etc. The third member is a man, and the fourth member is a woman caring for an elderly parent. Otherwise, the roles are interchangeable.

If a group is uncertain at first how to conduct a meeting, they may wish to begin by actually trying this role play. To do so immediately reveals its dramatic limitations. But as a means of easing general apprehension, or in some instances even relieving some real fear about being "judged," this has often proved to be a very helpful exercise.

Leader: Let us begin with prayer. Most gracious God, we are grateful once again to be in communion with each other and to meet in the name of Jesus Christ. We have journeyed for another week as your disciples, and we come now to give an account, to you and to one another, for the steps we have taken along the way. Be with us, we pray, in the power of your Holy Spirit. Give us fresh insight into our opportunities for service; give us humility to accept our shortcomings; give us grace to love and care for one another. In the name of Jesus Christ, Amen.
Let us now recite the covenant together.
(Here the group would read through its covenant.)
We'll begin with an act of devotion, the clause on prayer. You'll remember we missed it last week because we cut short our meeting to visit with the Amnesty International representative. "I will set aside a time for private prayer each day, and I will also pray with my family or friends." Let me begin with myself. Last week I could have reported much more positively than I can this week. Maybe

that's because we missed it last time. My set time for prayer is in the morning, and I have been faithful in that. But family prayer remains weak. In the evening, when we have agreed to hold family prayers, things seem to get away from me. The day doesn't come to a close: it tends to "fizzle out" in front of the television. I prayed on my own every day, but had family prayers only once.

(To First Member): And how about you? Were you faithful in your prayer life this week?

First Member: No, I'm afraid I wasn't either. Though my difficulty is exactly the opposite of yours. I am in a firm routine now of spending the closing minutes of the day in prayer and devotional reading. The trouble is that I am not a morning person.

Fifth Member: I know the feeling.

First Member: I'm not really "with it" when I stagger out of bed. By the time I'm awake, there seems to be no time to do anything except rush off to work. I've tried to set a time aside later in the morning, but there are twenty people in the office, so I really have to make the evening my priority.

Leader: That's fine. It's important to have a time of serious prayer when there are no other distractions, and the evening is as good a time as any. But a short prayer in the morning is helpful too. The new hymnal has quite a number of very good prayers, and some of them are well worth learning by heart. You might try one or two of them early in the day, until you can think straight!

(General group laughter, including First Member.)

(To Second Member): Tell us about your prayer life this week.

Second Member: Daily prayer comes easily to me. I've had a regular routine for years. I find that God reaches me in all sorts of ways during the day. But the best times I have are in the evenings, when I can go through my prayer list. I find that a lot of people ask me to pray for them, and it helps to have them listed so that I don't forget anyone.

Leader: That's fine. But I wonder whether you might ask one or two of your friends to join you for prayer once or twice a week? You seem to have a large prayer list, and it may be that some of the people you pray for would appreciate sharing with you in person. It might also help you in your own prayer life.

(To Third Member): And how about you?

Third Member: Not much to tell, I'm afraid.

Leader: Did you have any difficulties or problems?

Third Member: Not really.

Leader: Just something you have to keep working at.

Third Member: That's right.

Leader (to Fourth Member): How about your prayer life this week?

Fourth Member: Yes and no.

Leader: Oh? Tell us more! *(smiling).*

Fourth Member: I didn't feel it as quality prayer. I seemed to wander, and I never felt I was in a proper attitude of prayer. Even when I prayed with my family, I found myself thinking of other things.

Leader: But you at least *began* to pray. You did try.

Fourth Member: Yes, I tried.

Leader: Then you fulfilled the clause—you're the first person so far this week.

Fourth Member: What do you mean?

Leader: Our covenant states that we will pray each day, privately, and with family or friends. You are the only one who at least has attempted this each day. Whether or not our prayers feel good is not important. What matters is that we are open to God's grace. Don't think your time was wasted. You prayed.

(To Fifth Member): Were you faithful in prayer this week?

Fifth Member: Almost—on all but two days. I've been using the Job and Shawchuck book, *A Guide to Prayer,*[48] and it has really helped me. It has also helped me pray for people throughout the world, and especially those in the Third World. *(To Second Member)* I think you would find this helpful too, because it focuses on so many different areas for prayer, and has a lot of excerpts from the spiritual classics of the church.

Second Member: Thank you, I'll see if I can get hold of a copy. Of course, my prayer lists are so detailed that I'm not sure I could pack anything more into them. But at least I will have a look at a copy and see if . . .

Leader (interjecting): Good. But we have some other clauses in the covenant to get through, and we must press on. Let's turn now to acts of compassion, and the clause that reads: "I will give four hours each month to helping the disadvantaged in my community."

I remember when we adopted this clause, I was one of those who argued for four hours each week. But as you know, I haven't even kept up with four hours a month. I did make a commitment last week—finally—to spend a night at the shelter for the homeless, which should get me caught up a little.

(To Second Member): And how about you?

Second Member: Yes, I am up to date with my covenant. I help with Meals on Wheels twice a week, and that logs more than twenty hours a month for me.

Leader: Well done. You really do set the pace for us in this clause. It gives us something to aim for. You need to know that.

Second Member: Thank you.

Leader (to Third Member): Have you logged your four hours yet this month?

Third Member: Not yet. I was all set to do an evening at the homeless shelter, but I came down with the flu and couldn't go. I've given several neighbors a hand with various things, but that doesn't really count as disadvantaged, does it? *(General group silence.)* No, I thought not. Anyway, I'm limited to evenings and weekends, of course, because of my work. But I'll keep looking for an opportunity to get my hours in. One thing's for sure: With this clause, I won't forget.

Leader: You're right. It's been a real stickler for most of us; and sometimes I get so tired of saying I still haven't done it. Then I ask myself where I would be if I didn't have to answer for it each week. And I know what the answer is: I wouldn't even be *bothered* that I'm not doing anything. At least this way I'm aware of how little I'm doing for people in need.

(Turns to Fourth Member expectantly.)

Fourth Member: Well, as you know, I'm really tied to the house looking after my mother. It's very difficult to get out, because there's hardly anyone I can ask to stay with her. So I'm afraid I haven't put in my hours either.

Leader: And I'm afraid I disagree. I think you put in more hours than the rest of us put together; because if your mother is not disadvantaged, I don't know who is.

First Member: That's right. We should probably let you pass on this clause each week. *(General group affirmation.)*

Fourth Member: You're all very kind to say this. But I'm still going to look for a way to help some other people in need.

Leader (to Fifth Member): And where do you stand?

Fifth Member: At a considerable disadvantage, I'm sorry to say. *(Some group laughter.)* No, I have not yet locked into anything. But I'll keep reporting until I do.

Leader: Now let's turn to an act of worship: "I will receive the sacrament of Holy Communion each week." I know we can all give a positive answer here, because we agreed to attend early morning eucharist last Sunday, and we were all there. So rather than go around the circle, I'm just going to ask if there are any thoughts we have to share about the service.

Second Member: I was really moved by the time of open prayer we had after the message. There were so many needs expressed, and so much support from the people who were there. I really felt God's presence.

Fifth Member: As the pastor said the words of consecration, I remembered the time I was in Tiberias three years ago, by the Sea of Galilee. I'll never forget seeing that lake in the early morning sunlight. Taking the sacrament now always reminds me that Jesus was human. He actually walked those shores, and ate and drank with his disciples. He was part of our race. He *is* part of our race, and our planet.

First Member: The silence impressed me most. The sermon was short. . . .

Fifth Member: Amen!

First Member (smiling and continuing) . . . and then we were given time to think about it, and to reflect on the scripture readings. Being silent in company with other people is powerful. I wish we did it more often.

(General group silence.)

Leader: Any other comments? Then we'll go on to acts of justice. Of course, we may all soon be involved with Amnesty International.[49] I must confess I was not at all sure about asking their local representative to come and talk to us last week. I knew we needed to do something more specific—but actually getting down to where the rubber hits the road? Well, to be honest, I was a little nervous. But after hearing what she had to say, I'm much more convinced. We agreed to think it over very carefully for a couple of weeks, so this is really for next week's meeting. But I know already what I'm going to do. I'm going to get on board. Still, back to the clause for this week: "When I am aware of injustice to others, I will not remain silent."

(To First Member): Anything to report?

First Member: Not this week—at least, nothing that comes to mind.

Leader: O.K. *(To Second Member):* How about you?

Second Member: Nothing that I have been able to act on yet. But I did get a strong prompting from the Holy Spirit. It was this morning, actually, as I was eating breakfast. I suddenly realized that the choice was all mine, and it was what *not* to eat. Then I thought of the millions throughout the world, my brothers and sisters, whose choice this morning was very different. Their choice was whether to eat the little they had, or share it with the rest of their families— if they had anything to eat at all, that is.

I realized the terrible injustice, and that I was contributing to it by eating while they starve. I don't know what I am going to do about it yet. But I would like the group to keep me accountable for doing *something*.

Leader: Very well. Whoever leads next week, please make a note of that. We'll ask you about it.

(To Third Member): Did you encounter any injustices this week?

Third Member: Yes, I did. And I'm afraid I didn't speak out or do anything. At work last Friday, I was on the sixth floor of that new building in the square, and I heard an argument coming from down below. Come to find it was some Vietnamese who wanted to get the contract for cleaning the building. It's almost finished, as you know, and these people were quick off the mark. Seems they were offering a good price, but the contract had gone without bids to the company that does all the other buildings in town. Now I know that these Vietnamese do a good job. I've put in carpets where they do the cleaning, and they're still like new two years later. I *could* have gone down to put in a word for them. But I figured it was six floors down, and what good would it do? It hit me that night. I should have gone down. I should have said something. They were not getting a fair shake. I blew it.

Leader (after a short silence): Thank you for that.

(To Fourth Member): Any injustices this week?

Fourth Member: Well, I'm not sure this counts. You see, I think I was the one at the receiving end. I've had a really bad week. It's my mother. She keeps saying that I've not been a good daughter to her all these years, but that's not true. I know I may not have done all that I should, but I look after her around the clock. I do her washing, I take her to the doctor, I get all her prescriptions. And really, my own life comes second because of her. Yet once again last week she accused me of being ungrateful to her. I don't know whether what I'm feeling is self-pity, or whether I am being treated unjustly. Deep down, I don't *think* I'm resenting her. But every time she says this, I have doubts all over again.

Leader: This really seems to have upset you, doesn't it? Tell you what we might do. We have the rest of the covenant to get through right now, but perhaps one or two of us could stay behind after the meeting, and talk some more about it. Would anyone else have time to stay for a while? *(First Member nods, and Fifth Member indicates willingness to stay also.)* Good. Let's do that, then. *(To Fifth Member):* And how about this clause for you?

Fifth Member: I've had a rather strong prompting too, and I'm afraid I'm going to pass it on to all of us.

Leader: Go ahead.

Fifth Member: It dawned on me after our last board meeting how much we are spending in the church on new fixtures and carpets. *(To Third Member)* Sorry about this, 'cause I know you have the contract. But I have to say it.

Third Member: That's all right.

Fifth Member: If we gave away even half of what we are raising for all this renovation, we could quadruple our annual giving to world hunger. *(To Second Member)* Here's something you might be able to do about *your* prompting, because my prompting is that we should go to the board as a group, and make this as a motion.

Third Member: I'm with you in principle, but I don't think it'll do any good. That board makes up its mind, and that's that.

Leader: Perhaps. But you never can tell—and at least we can let them know *why* we are making the motion—that one of us has been prompted by the Holy Spirit, and the rest of us are in agreement. At least, I don't see anyone disagreeing.

(There is a general nod of approval.)

Fine. Then we need to know how many of us can attend the board meeting, and who will make the motion. We can decide that after we conclude.

(Other clauses in the covenant would then be taken in turn at the leader's discretion, following the same format of question and answer and feedback.)

Leader: That concludes our covenant for this week. Now we come to the personal clauses. I don't recall any from last week. *(The group indicates agreement.)* Do any of us wish to make a personal covenant for next week, then?

First Member: Yes, I do. I will covenant with God and make myself accountable to the group for not losing my temper at work next week.

Fifth Member: I have one, too. I covenant with God and hold myself accountable to the group for making a $100 donation to world hunger this week.

Leader: Thank you both for those commitments. Who is going to lead next week?

Third Member: I will.

Leader: Fine. Don't forget these two personal clauses. We'll meet here next week, same time, same place. Now let us have our closing time of prayer. Are there any special concerns?

(Members of the group offer several concerns: for the fourth member and her mother; for the Vietnamese cleaners and all immigrants who find it difficult to gain acceptance; and for guidance in presenting the motion to the church board.)

Leader (to the First Member, who is also the Convener of the group): Perhaps it would be a good idea if you could let the pastor and the board chairperson know that we will be coming to make this motion. *(To everyone):* How many of us can be there next Thursday for the board meeting?

(Three members indicate that they can be there.)

Good. Let's get there half an hour early so we can agree on what to say.

(To Fourth Member, along with First and Fifth Members): Now, why don't we go and get a cup of coffee somewhere, and talk about you and your mother? This really must be a burden for you.

Conclusion

TWO WARNINGS AND A PROMISE

The commitment made by members of covenant discipleship groups almost always causes an infectious exuberance, and in the first few weeks of the meetings there are many positive experiences. The hunger for this sort of firm accountability is real, and it will also be accompanied by the fascination for something new and exciting, from which none of us is altogether immune.

As new groups are formed and begin to meet, therefore, it is important to issue two warnings—and along with the warnings, a promise.

THE "DOLDRUMS"

The catechesis of being accountable for aspects of discipleship, which have hitherto been neglected or taken for granted, gives each group a wealth of insight and challenge during the first two months of meeting together. After three or four months, however, a sense of routine sets in. The questions seem to become mechanical. Answers lack spontaneity, and members begin to question the validity and usefulness of the whole exercise.

It should be clearly stated to new groups that this time of "doldrums" is to be expected, and for two reasons. The most immediate cause is the wish to turn to something new when the novelty of the groups has worn off. In part this is reflective of our culture's preoccupation with self-fulfillment, and it should be firmly resisted. Indeed, withdrawing from religious "junk food" is one of the most important functions of covenant discipleship groups.

There is a deeper spiritual reason for the "doldrums," however, which can best be described as "getting a second wind." Most churchgoers today are out of practice when it comes to accountable discipleship. Many have allowed themselves to become spectators in church, watching and perhaps admiring those who seem to be committed to their faith, though not really wishing to join them in the work of Jesus Christ. Now that they are in a covenant discipleship group, there is no avoiding the challenge of discipleship. While this is exhilarating at first, there comes a times when the routine of the task begins to take hold, and when the daily grind requires stamina.

As a group gets this second wind, it should be explained that this is exactly what covenant discipleship is all about. It is an agreement to watch over one another. We are in covenant, not merely to share the high points of our journey, important though these are, but much more to sustain and support each other in the midst of the routine and the commonplace.

If a group remains faithful to its covenant through these "doldrums," it is not long before the rough and tumble of living in the world brings the members to realize even more profoundly the value of this common bond. Such times of apparent aimlessness are no more than a test of the commitment they have made, a searching and tempering of their discipleship, a moving away from self-serving interests to those which are Christ-serving. It is a form of spiritual growth well attested in the history of the Christian faith; but groups need to know about it at the outset, and to be ready for it.

COMPLACENCY

New groups should also be warned against the danger of becoming complacent about their accountability. When this happens, it usually takes the form of thoughtless, or worse, dishonest answers. These are very infectious, putting the group at a serious disadvantage, and having an adverse effect on the meetings. Groups should know in advance that this is a real danger to their purpose and well-being.

Suggestions have been made in the preceding chapters about ways in which the leader can address such problems each week. But a general word of advice, based on many reports received from groups, is that if complacency is a problem in a group, time and again the reason proves to be procrastination. The members have reached a point where the grace of God is impelling them to take another step in their discipleship, be it in the area of compassion, justice, worship, or devotion. But they are putting it off; they are holding out against grace. Therefore grace is not flowing as it should in their weekly meetings. In a word, they are being *disobedient*—the very thing Wesley warned would shipwreck a Christian's discipleship.

A group suffering from complacency, therefore, should ask itself a very candid question: What are we not doing that we have been clearly prompted to do by the Holy Spirit? The answer will probably be very simple, very obvious, and very do-able. So do it!

THE PROMISE OF GRACE

Last, it is important to stress to new groups that they must expect the grace of God to invade their lives in new ways. That is not only a promise. Indeed, as we have noted, it can also be a threat. For now that they are making themselves accountable for the means through which grace can flow, flow it will—and in ways for which they are probably not quite ready.

It means, for example, that as members become disciplined in the General Rule of Discipleship—in acts of compassion, devotion, worship, and justice—they will consciously experience the love and power of God as never before. Prayer will be more efficacious in their lives. Worship will be more inspiring. Service to others will be more fulfilling. Justice will be more compelling. Likewise, spiritual promptings and warnings will be unnervingly direct. There will be a stronger call to work for the new age of Jesus Christ, as well as new hope in its ultimate fulfillment, on earth as in heaven.

All this will happen, because being accountable for our discipleship is far from an exercise in self-improvement. It is opening ourselves to the gracious initiatives of the Holy Spirit, as promised to us by God in Christ Jesus. And John Wesley's words still ring loud and clear, calling us to accountable discipleship:

> We go on from grace to grace, while we are careful to 'abstain from all appearance of evil', and are 'zealous of good works', 'as we have opportunity doing good to all men'; while we

walk in all his ordinances blameless, therein worshipping him in spirit and in truth; while we take up our cross and deny ourselves in every pleasure that does not lead us to God.[50]

Endnotes

1. *The United Methodist Hymnal* (Nashville: The United Methodist Publishing House, 1989), #378.

2. "The Incarnate One," from Edwin Muir, *Collected Poems* (London: Faber and Faber, 1963), p. 228.

3. *The United Methodist Hymnal,* #378.

4. *The Bicentennial Edition of the Works of John Wesley, Volume 9: The Methodist Societies: History, Nature, and Design,* ed. Rupert E. Davies (hereafter *Wesley's Works*) (Nashville: Abingdon Press, 1989), p. 69.

5. *The Works of John Wesley,* 14 vols., ed. Thomas Jackson (hereafter Jackson, *Works*), (Grand Rapids, Michigan: Baker Book House, 1979), 8:300.

6. Albert C. Outler, ed., *John Wesley* (New York: Oxford University Press, 1964), p. vii.

7. Jackson, *Works,* 13:230.

8. *Wesley's Works, Volume 25: Letters I,* ed. Frank Baker (New York: Oxford University Press, 1980), pp. 144ff.

9. Frank Baker, *John Wesley and the Church of England* (Nashville: Abingdon Press, 1970), pp. 4-5.

10. *Wesley's Works, Volume 26: Letters II,* ed. Frank Baker (New York: Oxford University Press, 1982), p. 206.

11. *Wesley's Works,* 25:615-16.

12. Jackson, *Works,* 8:248.

13. Jackson, *Works,* 13:226.

14. *Wesley's Works, Volumes 1-4: Sermons I (1-33); II (34-70); III (71-114): IV (115-151),* ed. Albert C. Outler (Nashville: Abingdon Press, 1984-87), 3:64ff.

15. David Lowes Watson, *The Early Methodist Class Meeting* (Nashville: Discipleship Resources, 1985), p. 69.

16. *Wesley's Works,* 9:77-8.

17. Colin W. Williams, *John Wesley's Theology Today* (Nashville: Abingdon Press, 1960), pp. 72-3.

18. *Wesley's Works, Volume 7: A Collection of Hymns for the Use of the*

People called Methodists, ed. Franz Hildebrandt & Oliver A. Becker-legge, asst. James Dale (Nashville: Abingdon Press, 1989), p. 82.

19. Jackson, *Works,* 8:322-23.

20. "The Nature, Design, and General Rules, of the United Societies, in London, Bristol, King's-wood, and Newcastle upon Tyne," in *Wesley's Works,* 9:69.

21. Ibid., pp. 69, 70, 261.

22. Ibid., p. 434.

23. Jackson, *Works,* 8:322 ff.

24. Ibid., p. 324.

25. *Wesley's Works,* 3:385.

26. Watson, *Class Meeting,* pp. 109-10.

27. *The Letters of John Wesley,* ed. John Telford, 8 vols. (London: Epworth Press, 1931), 4:194.

28. Watson, *Class Meeting,* p. 131.

29. Baker, *John Wesley and the Church of England,* pp. 160-79.

30. Jackson, *Works,* 8:299.

31. *Wesley's Works,* 3:64.

32. *Wesley's Works,* 9:69.

33. *United Methodist Hymnal,* #438.

34. *Wesley's Works,* 1:415-43, 2:186-201.

35. *Wesley's Works,* 7:77-8.

36. *John and Charles Wesley: Selected Writings and Hymns,* ed. Frank Whaling (New York: Paulist Press, 1981), p. 139.

37. *Wesley's Works,* 2:37-8.

38. *Wesley's Works,* 9:72.

39. Jackson, *Works,* 8:300.

40. See above, n.1.

41. Geoffrey Wainwright, *Doxology: The Praise of God in Worship, Doctrine, and Life* (New York: Oxford University Press, 1980).

42. For example: John Baillie, *A Diary of Private Prayer* (New York: Scribner's, 1936), reprinted many times; and Rueben P. Job and Norman Shawchuck, *A Guide to Prayer for Ministers and Other Servants* (Nashville: The Upper Room, 1983), already a modern classic.

43. Oswald Chambers, *My Utmost for His Highest* (New York: Dodd, Mead & Company, 1935), pp. 12-13.

44. Lisa Grant, *Branch Groups: Covenant Discipleship for Youth* (Nashville: Discipleship Resources, 1988), p. 17.

45. Kim A. Hauenstein-Mallet and Kenda Creasy Dean, *Covenants on Campus: Covenant Discipleship Groups for College and University Students* (Nashville: Discipleship Resources, 1991), pg. 75.

46. Ibid., p. 76.

47. See Thomas H. Groome, *Christian Religious Education: Sharing Our Story and Vision* (San Francisco: Harper & Row, 1980), pp. 26-27.

48. See above, n.42.

49. The purpose of Amnesty International, 322 Eighth Avenue, New York, NY 10001, is "to work impartially to free prisoners of conscience (men, women, and children jailed solely for their beliefs or ethnic origins, provided they have neither used nor advocated violence), to ensure fair trials for all political prisoners, and to abolish torture and executions."

50. *Wesley's Works*, 2:160.

Resources

Covenant Discipleship: Christian Formation through Mutual Accountability by David Lowes Watson.

This new manual advances the guidelines for covenant discipleship groups by incorporating learnings of the past decade from groups in the United States and around the world. **(#DR091)**

Class Leaders: Recovering a Tradition by David Lowes Watson.

Taking the later Methodist class meeting as a model, this book shows how class leaders can foster the discipleship of a pastoral subdivision of the congregation. **(#DR092)**

Forming Christian Disciples: The Role of Covenant Discipleship and Class Leaders in the Congregation by David Lowes Watson.

This third volume gives the procedures for introducing and sustaining covenant discipleship groups, and explains the role of class leaders in the congregation. **(#DR093)**

Covenants on Campus: Covenant Discipleship Groups for College and University Students by Kim Hauenstein-Mallet and Kenda Creasy Dean.

Written especially for campus ministers, college-town church leaders, and college students, this book explains the values of shared Christian discipleship according to biblical principles. **(#DR099)**

The Early Methodist Class Meeting: Its Origins and Significance by David Lowes Watson. Foreword by Albert C. Outler.

This volume provides the historical background of the early class meeting, including a theological assessment of its place in Wesley's leadership of the Methodist movement. **(#DR017)**

Wesley Speaks on Christian Vocation by Paul Wesley Chilcote.

Using Wesley's own writings as a source of inspiration, Chilcote addresses the deep vocational questions that shape the life of the faithful Christian disciple. **(#DR041)**

Discípulos Responsables por David Lowes Watson. Prólogo por Mortimer Arias.

Este libro presenta una excelente base para la formación, desarrollo, y acción de grupos de discípulos responsables en nuestra iglesia. **(#F023B)**

Branch Groups: Covenant Discipleship for Youth by Lisa Grant.
An adaptation of the early Methodist class meeting for the youth of today, branch groups enable young people to practice the basics of discipleship in covenant with one another.

Christian Formation Brochure
Copies of this brochure are available for distribution in congregations and other settings, and may be purchased in multiples of 100.

Covenant Discipleship Quarterly
The *Quarterly* is an important supplement to the handbook, *Covenant Discipleship*. It features articles about Christian discipleship in different contexts, and reports from covenant discipleship groups around the world.

Journal for Covenant Discipleship
Available in English and Spanish. The *Journal*, with a separate page for each week of the year, provides a place for group members to record their experiences and insights, enabling them to give a more meaningful account of their discipleship at their weekly meetings.

Both the *Quarterly* and the *Journal* can be ordered from the **Office of Covenant Discipleship and Christian Formation, General Board of Discipleship, P.O. Box 840, Nashville, TN 37202-0840. (615) 340-7010.**

NOTES

NOTES

NOTES

NOTES

April 2

11 am

Jefferson